British
CHARCUTERIE

British

CHARCUTERIE

*Traditional pork cookery from
Kentish Gammon to Lincolnshire Chine*

◆

JENNIE REEKIE

WARD LOCK LIMITED · LONDON

First published in Great Britain in
1988 by Ward Lock Limited,
8 Clifford Street, London W1X 1RB,
an Egmont Company

Designed by Ann Thompson
Black and white illustrations by
John Spencer
Colour illustrations by
Diana Leadbetter
Text filmset in 11/13pt Century
Schoolbook by M & R Computerised
Typesetting Ltd., Grimsby
Printed and bound in Spain by
Cayfosa, Barcelona.

British Library Cataloguing in
Publication Data
Reekie, Jennie
British charcuterie
1. Food. British pork dishes. Recipes
I. Title
641.6 '44' 0941

ISBN 0-7063-6680-8

CONTENTS

'Look at pork. There's a subject.
If you want a subject, look at pork.'
Charles Dickens, *Great Expectations*

INTRODUCTION

Up until the Industrial Revolution, pork was the only meat the majority of peasants ever ate. Sometimes it would be supplemented by a farmyard chicken or a snared rabbit or, if they were prepared to risk their luck, some poached venison or hare. The pig was the cottager's friend and ally for, if nurtured well through the summer and autumn, they would be assured of a little meat in winter when food of any kind was exceedingly scarce.

Travel was difficult and hazardous, so people did not venture far unless the journey was essential. It is, therefore, hardly surprising that even in as small a country as the British Isles, regional differences in food preparation developed.

The overall pattern and methods were the same in that hams were cured, pies were baked and chopped meat was pushed into skins to make sausages. However, the ways in which this was done varied considerably in different parts of the country. One has only to think of the difference between an unsmoked green York ham and that of a heavily-smoked Suffolk sweetcure ham; or the fat coils of a Cumberland sausage against the vivid green links of the Lincolnshire. In short, we have a wealth of great regional specialities which are rapidly in danger of being lost and forgotten in these days of mass-produced, mass-marketed food.

'Everything is used except the squeak' was what they used to say, and truly not one little bit of the pig was wasted.

As soon as the pig had been slaughtered, the skin would either be singed or scalded to remove the hair. The hams, or legs, would be cut off and put to dry salt together with the sides, or flitches and either with or without the shoulder. This, together with the hand, might either be kept and roasted or used to make sausages. The prime cut of all, the tenderloin or fillet, would either be kept by the

owner of the pig or given as a present to a highly respected member of the family. Frequently, it would be sent as a gift or form part of the rent to the landlord.

Having dispensed with the main joints, the head, trotters and possibly the tail would be used for brawn. Often the tail was added to another dish, such as rabbit stew, in order to give it added flavour. The heart and liver might be eaten on their own, or with the rest of the pluck i.e. the lungs and spleen, be made into faggots or haslet. Sometimes they would be cooked and used for pig's fry, and the kidneys would be cooked up for breakfast the following morning.

The intestines would be very carefully washed. The smaller ones would then be used as a casing for sausages, the large ones for black pudding and the still larger ones for chitterlings. Any rind that was left would be made into pork scratchings and all the fat would be rendered down for lard while the blood was used to make black puddings.

In villages, it was normal for the pigs to be killed in rotation. People shared the offal and fresh meat and this ensured a continuous supply of meat for everyone from September right through until Christmas. The last pig to go would be the boar, having done his duty by the village breeding sows. He would be used for the Christmas feasting.

For many years it has been fashionable to denigrate British food by referring to it as some of the worst in the world. Some of this criticism is grossly unfair. It cannot be disputed that the social upheavals brought about by World War I resulted in some very poor cooks being employed in restaurants and private houses. Their food had very little to recommend it and comments like Somerset Maugham's much quoted, 'If you would eat well in England you must eat breakfast three times a day' were not without foundation.

Country people, on the other hand, who did not rely on cooks and did their own cooking, were not affected in the same way. They continued using the same recipes that their parents and grand-parents had used before them. It is from this source that by far the greater number of recipes in this book come. Not from the poorly-cooked, pseudo-French fare of the second-class restaurant which did so much to harm the reputation of our food. Traditional old-fashioned British food is something we can, and should be, justly proud of.

When it comes to recommending butchers, shops or suppliers, there are bound to be outcries because I have not mentioned somebody's local butcher who makes the best sausages in the world, or cures hams magnificently. For this I can only apologize, but to visit every pork butcher and sausagemaker would be a lifetime's work! The ones written about I have either just stumbled upon or were recommended to me by friends and acquaintances or I read about in other books and magazines.

I have thoroughly enjoyed researching this book. I have eaten a lot of very good food and found out some fascinating bits of history and culture about my own country which I did not know before. Above all, I have had the privilege and pleasure of meeting so many kind, interesting people who were very generous with their time and advice, for which I can only say 'Thank you'.

Jennie Reekie

CHAPTER ONE

A PLACE IN THE HISTORY BOOKS

◆

The importance of the pig in British rural economy right up until the beginning of this century cannot be overstated. It is no coincidence that children's money boxes always used to be, and frequently still are, various forms of pig and that we use expressions like 'bringing home the bacon' and 'piggy bank'. For many, the pig really was their bank and if any ill befell him, the family could be in severe financial trouble. The pig was often known as 'the gentleman who pays the rent' for he would be used during the summer months to obtain credit. Then, come autumn when he was killed, the creditor could either be repaid in money or, more likely, with a piece of pork.

The pig was first domesticated as early as the late Neolithic or early Bronze Age. He would have borne little resemblance to today's porkers having been quite rangy and with long legs. Indeed, it was not until 200 years ago, when the European breeds were crossed with Chinese pigs, that he began to change and resemble his current shape.

The success of the pig as a domestic animal is due to several factors. The early pig, first cousin to the wild boar, was a hardy creature and easy to raise. Like man, pigs are omnivorous, they will eat meat as well as vegetable matter such as grasses and cereals. In fact, they will eat just about anything that is given to them! Consequently, they are not difficult to feed, and they fatten more quickly than other animals reared for meat such as sheep, goats and cattle. Pigs also have the facility to breed easily and interbreed, which has gradually led to the evolution of the twentieth century breeds. The only thing the pig does not relish is being asked to travel for long distances. This in part accounts for his lack of popularity amongst the previously nomadic tribes of the Middle East.

During their occupation of the British Isles, although the Romans enjoyed hunting wild boar, they also encouraged the production of domestic pigs. They were particularly partial to suckling pig which always featured on the menu at any banquet or celebration dinner. Gaul hams from France were regularly despatched to Rome and in an excavation at Winchester they found a 'tray set with cutlery for a meal, a pig's trotter and a Bath Chap'.

Not long ago I had to prepare a dish of suckling pig for a film about Roman food which I found rather macabre. A pair of roast suckling pigs had to curl up to each other on a vast platter as if they were asleep, while their intestines were stuffed to resemble straw for them to lie on! Whatever the merits (or demerits) of such a dish, the Roman passion for stuffing intestines taught the ancient Britons the invaluable art of sausage-making, including black pudding and haggis.

The word 'sausage' stems from the Latin *salsa*, or to salt, as does the French *saucission* and the Italian *salami*. Clearly, the original sausages were heavily salted and possibly smoked in order to preserve them. What is perhaps surprising is that we were not left with a tradition of making air-dried sausages such as salami, but our climate must take the blame for that. The damp atmosphere of the winter months, when curing was always carried out, is not conducive to successful air-drying. The drier the atmosphere the better, and the best salamis are still produced in the mountainous regions of Europe.

Not a great deal is known about Saxon food but records show that both the Saxons and the Celts salted pork. The Exe and Creddy valleys boasted large herds of swine and in the eastern counties of England, sheep, pigs and goats were raised. The main concentration of pigs was in areas where there were large tracts of forest. Here the pigs could forage in autumn, the chief fattening time, on acorns and beech nuts, also known as beech mast.

Under the Anglo Saxons, some of the peasants were allowed to fatten their pigs for free, but after the Norman invasion tithes always had to be paid for the privilege. Called *denera* in Anglo Saxon England and *pannage* under the Normans, this was a system which endured right through to the Elizabethan era. By the reign of Henry VIII it had to be paid in money, a penny or a penny halfpenny per year being about the average charge. At the time of King Alfred, however, payment was in kind according to

the fatness of the pig. One third of the animal with three fingers of fat on its body, one quarter of those with two fingers but only one fifth of those with a thumb of fat!

The importance of this as a source of revenue to the feudal landowners can be seen. King Ine (AD 640) passed a law which imposed penalties for burning mast-bearing trees. The value of a tree was governed by how many pigs could find shelter under it. In the Domesday Book, much mention is made of 'woodland for swine' and the value of a wood was determined by how many pigs it could support. In order to prevent the pigs doing extensive damage to young saplings and tree roots by foraging for food, the *denera* or *pannage* season was a limited one. In Anglo-Saxon England it began on 29 August and lasted until New Year's Eve.

Most families at this time would have kept a pig or two. In order that the pigs did not prevent them from going about their daily duties, during the *pannage* season they would employ the services of a swineherd. He would go around the village in the early morning collecting the pigs and then return them at night, but sometimes he would even sleep out in the forest with them in a makeshift hut. In the small dwellings in which the majority of peasants lived, the pig had another useful function. In order to prevent fire from breaking out in the huts, laws were passed both by King Alfred and later by William the Conqueror, insisting that the fires used inside the homes for cooking be extinguished and the ashes thrown out by nightfall. Interestingly, this gives us the word 'curfew', coming from the French *couvre-feu*. The temperature in these crudely-made buildings would then rapidly drop and the warmth of the pig's body would have been an invaluable source of heat during the night.

By the end of the fourteenth century, the vast herds of swine which had characterized Anglo Saxon and Norman times had diminished. Many of the forests had been cut down to provide arable land and there was no longer an unlimited supply of fodder for them. They continued, however, to be reared in much the same way as before though the Tudor author, Thomas Tusser, indicates that by then the pannage season might have been lengthened.

'At Hallowmas (1 November) slaughter time soon cometh in;
And then doth the husbandmen's feasting begin.
From that time to Candlemas (2 February) weekly kill some;
Ham offal for household the better shall come.'

He also pointed out that it was extremely beneficial if there was a good strong wind in October to blow down the beech nuts.

'October good blast
to blowe the hog mast'.

Despite this apparently efficient means of fattening pigs on beech nuts and acorns, there would appear to have been dangers if they were fed on acorns out of season as he gave this warning:

'Though plenty of acornes, the porkling to fat,
not taken in season, may perish by that;
If rattling or swelling get once to the throte,
thou loosest they porkling, a crowne to a grote.'

Throughout the late Medieval and Tudor periods, brawn was one of the most important dishes served at any feast or banquet, culminating in the Christmas brawn made from boar's head. In the thirteenth century, it was always served at the end of the feast. By the time of the enthronement of Archbishop Nevill in 1467 during the reign of Edward IV, it had become a first course. While some brawn would have been produced from domesticated pigs, that of wild boar was considered superior for special occasions such as Christmas.

Wild boar was still quite common in Britain until the fifteenth century, but indiscriminate hunting caused it to become completely extinct on these islands by the seventeenth century. It is still hunted in Europe, especially in parts of Germany and the Sologne in France. Recently, a few boars have been reintroduced to Britain. They are being crossed with Tamworth pigs to provide boar meat, and are being raised on a few farms in England, Wales and Scotland.

Although it was not until 1760, when Robert Bakewell crossed the British pig with a Chinese strain that the enormously fat pigs of the nineteenth century were produced, the domesticated pig of earlier centuries was still quite a fat animal. Current fashions demand a leaner pig but in those days the fat of the pig was as valuable as the lean. Every last bit would be rendered down to provide lard for cooking or for spreading thinly on bread when flavoured with rosemary, salt and pepper. Butter was a rare and expensive commodity and vegetable fats were unheard of.

In Medieval times, the candles for churches and some of the bigger houses were made from beeswax, but the general household candles were produced either from pork or mutton fat. For those on the land, the day started at dawn and ended at dusk and candles were considered an unnecessary luxury. However, in times of necessity, a simple one could be made using a little pork fat in a bowl with a strip of linen floating on the top of it.

Even during the seventeenth and eighteenth centuries, the hardness of the lean of the salt pork and the harshness of its flavour demanded plenty of fat to make it palatable. With little heat to warm them in winter and a lot of hard manual work expected of them, the peasants needed as much fat to keep them going as their limited means allowed. Sitting in our warm, centrally-heated homes, we may find steamed suet puddings heavy fare, but for our ancestors they were very necessary. Even the gentry needed more food than we do in winter as the body expends a considerable amount of energy just in keeping warm.

This remained the case throughout the nineteenth century. In 1822, William Cobbett felt that 'if a hog be more than a year old he is the better for it. Make him fat by all means. If he can walk two or three hundred yards at a time, he is not well fatted. Lean bacon is the most wasteful thing that a family can use. In short, it is uneatable except by drunkards who want something to stimulate their sickly appetites'.

The ability to keep an animal through the winter greatly facilitated the production of specific bacon pigs. Hay had always been in existence, as well as cereals, but these had always been reserved for the horses and cattle. The importing of trefoil, clover and lucerne hay from the Netherlands during the eighteenth century meant that there was now more winter feed to go round, including some for the pigs.

As has been said, the introduction of the Eastern pig played an important role in the development of a more productive pig. It was at the end of the eighteenth century that many of the familiar British breeds started to develop. Instead of having prick ears like a wild boar, they now had the more familiar lop ears and generally became a heavier animal.

During the Industrial Revolution, when the country people left the land and flocked to the cities in their thousands, ways of feeding them had to be found. Families were no longer able to keep their own pig, although some indeed tried, and laws had to be introduced banning the keeping of pigs in urban areas. This is when commercial pig farming developed.

The rise of the commercial pig farm also saw the rise of the specialist pork butcher who has since done so much to safeguard regional specialities and the very best pork products. While some of these are in country towns and villages, the greater majority are in the Industrial towns of the Midlands and the north of England.

For those people who had remained on the land, life continued much as it always had. While there were few forests, the remaining pigs were kept on arable land or in small stys beside a cottage, and fed on kitchen waste and cereals. The sows, usually kept by the farmers, would farrow down (or give birth) at the beginning of the year. Even in Tudor times, Thomas Tusser talked about a pig farrowing in January. If they were lucky, they might have obtained a second litter from her. Cottagers would then purchase a weaner to rear through the spring and summer and kill it in late autumn when it had been fattened. Or they would keep it even longer if really fat bacon was required – a timeless cycle which continued well into the beginning of this century.

Since World War II, there have been dramatic changes in both pig breeding and farming. An exploding population, mainly urban-based, wanting plentiful supplies of cheap meat, coupled with what are now known to be misconstrued ideas about just how much protein the body requires, made successive governments demand that farmers increase production.

There were only two ways in which this could be done. One, by improving the productivity of the pig and two, more intensive farming. The improvement (or, as some would have it, ruination) of the pig was brought about by the increased use of early-maturing pigs, such as the Large White, which had already attained prominence in the early part of the century, and also by crossing them with the Scandinavian Landrace. For some time, pigs had been reared in large sheds or houses but various ways were found of rearing more in a limited space and on a concentrated diet. The result has been that in 1985 the total production of fresh pork was 732,000 tonnes and 204,000 tonnes of bacon.

Over the centuries, the pig has given so much to the British way of life, adapting himself as our lives and needs have changed and developed. At the intensive farm I visited, they send fifty young pigs up to a London hospital every fortnight. Only three or so of these may be found to be suitable, but the valves from their hearts can then be transplanted into those of young children. Really, what more could we ask of him?

CHAPTER TWO

MODERN PIG KEEPING AND PRODUCTION

◆

It is only too easy to be carried away by rather romantic notions of how pigs used to be kept in yesteryear. Certainly, at the beginning of this century and even after World War I, there were plenty of pigs kept in stys in small paddocks or orchards where they could forage around, eating windfall apples and acorns in the autumn. 'Haycorns' as A A Milne's Piglet called them.

Others, owned by cottagers with only a very limited amount of land, were not as fortunate. They rarely left their sty and only occasionally were allowed out on foraging trips, and that depended on the benevolence of the local landowner. The idea of intensive fattening is not new. Centuries ago Thomas Moufat recommended his reader to 'Shut up a young boar of a year and a half old, in a little room in harvest-time, feeding him on nothing but sweet whey and giving him every morning clean straw to lie upon, but lay it not too thick, so before Christmas he will be sufficient brawned with continual laying and prove exceedingly fat, wholesome and sweet.'

Some pigs that were kept on farms lived almost entirely on a diet of excrement from the other farm animals, cattle and horses in particular. As animals definitely do tend to be 'tainted' by their fodder, one cannot imagine that these beasts were pork at their most delicious.

I say this because I feel that much of the criticism that is made of intensive or factory farmers seems a little unfair. True, the pigs do lead an 'unnatural' life in that they never go outside and live in large groups without a great deal of space, but the ones I saw all appeared clean, happy and healthy. If put under too much stress, they would simply drop down dead. True, the pigs used are hybrid crosses which have specifically been developed because they mature quickly, but these pigs also produce leaner pork which is what the public generally wants.

True, antibiotics are added to their feed because a form of pneumonia is ever-present and herds containing thousands of pigs would just be wiped out without its use. It is not, however, an antibiotic which is ever given to humans and the vast majority of farmers are responsible enough to cease using it fourteen days before slaughter; the recommended time. True, growth promoters are also added and one would really prefer it if they weren't, but these farms do produce lean meat at a very reasonable price.

At the other end of the spectrum are farms where the pigs are all old English stock, or 'rare breeds' as they are generally known. They have unadulterated food and live outside. However, even at

Heal's Farm in Devon, the best known of these establishments, they are kept inside for three months of the winter to conserve the pasture. In an ideal world, we would all prefer to eat pork that is reared along the Heal's Farm lines but it costs approximately double!

There are countless reasons for this. Quite apart from the obvious ones, such as the slower growth rate of the rare breeds like the Gloucester Old Spot (see above) and the fact that any animal that wanders around and takes exercise will need more food than one that doesn't. As one might expect, the rare breeds do not produce as many piglets as the more highly-developed Large White and Landrace, or crosses of these. Sows are also clumsy creatures and, when left to their own devices, they usually manage to squash a few of their piglets! So, the unit cost per piglet bred is considerably higher.

Many of the rare breeds became rare not only because of their comparatively slow maturity but because of public demand for leaner meat. One of the complaints often made about today's pork, especially by the older butchers, is that the lean is not firm and tends to weep. Fat absorbs much of the moisture giving firmer lean muscle and, many people feel, a superior flavour. The ratio of fat to lean is much higher in the rare breeds than in the hybrids, but if people only want to eat the lean meat, the fat has to be discarded. This is an expensive and wasteful system as the soap industry (the biggest user of surplus fat) is not a generous payer.

In between these two extreme methods of farming, there are others rearing pigs with slightly less intensity. Perhaps the sows live outside and the piglets are weaned a little later, instead of after three weeks which is fairly standard on an intensive unit.

There are commercial pigs living a 'free-range' lifestyle and some which are kept inside but are not fed with any hormones, growth promoters or antibiotics, unless they are actually ill. There are various computations, all of which in the final analysis are reflected in the price we pay for the meat. In theory, this means that everyone has a choice in the kind of meat they buy but, as we all know, in practice it means that only a certain section of society does. Whether we like it or not, for the foreseeable future the intensive farm is here to stay.

CHAPTER THREE

FRESH MEAT PRODUCTS

This chapter concentrates on all the best known fresh pork products i.e. sausages, pork pies, faggots and brawn and the different regional variations amongst them. A few products have been excluded, simply because they are neither as appetizing nor as interesting as many of their kind. Two which at least deserve a mention, however, are the Saveloy and Poloney.

I always connect saveloys with fish and chip shops as this was where they could always be found, before being usurped by chicken and battered bangers. Sadly, the average saveloy looked a great deal better than it tasted, being mostly seasoned cereal binder. A corruption of the French *cervelas* – brains – saveloys used to be made with the previously brined pluck of the pig, together with some lean pork. It was then hot-smoked and boiled and the saltpetre from the brining gave the skin its distinctive pink tinge.

Saveloys are sold fully cooked and can be eaten cold, but it is more normal to boil them – as one would a continental boiling sausage – and serve it hot. Ralph's butchers in Melton Mowbray do a good saveloy which is vacuum-packed so will keep for some time.

There appears to be some doubt as to whether the word 'Poloney' comes from Bologna or Polonia, but it would be true to say that whichever, it is not one of Britain's most distinguished pork products. It is a cooked sausage, often lightly hot-smoked and made with very finely-minced pork or a mixture of pork and beef, cereal and seasoning. The quality of it varies as the proportion of meat decreases and that of the cereal increases. Generally sold sliced, for serving cold with salad or as a sandwich filling, if well made as at Scott's in York, it can be surprisingly good.

SAUSAGES

Ever since the Romans taught us how to make sausages, we have been a nation of sausage lovers. We actually eat six billion of them a year! Queen Victoria was so fond of them that she laid down rules as to how they should be made in the royal households. The meat had to be chopped, not minced, so that none of the juices were squeezed out and the skins had to be filled by hand by pressing the mixture through a funnel with the thumbs. It was a time-consuming and laborious process as you can imagine.

Sausages were always a way of using the cheaper, fattier cuts such as shoulder and hand, as well as bits and pieces left over from butchering the meat. Many sausages would then be preserved by putting them up the chimney to smoke for four or five days. They would have been well seasoned with salt and possibly saltpetre as well. This is purported to be the origin of the word 'banger' in that saltpetre was also used for gunpowder. Others say that the word comes from the banging of the knife of the butcher's block as the butcher finely chopped the meat in the days before mincing machines.

While sausages virtually never contained the prime cuts such as the loin or the leg, what was used was proper meat unlike the contents of many of the commercial sausages these days. Ways have been found of 'mechanically recovering' the meat left on the bones by normal butchering. This is done by a battery of sharp knives which shear it off, together with all the sinew and gristle, and is known in the trade as 'slurry'. Rind is, for the most part, chemically emulsified so that it becomes soft enough to mince and add to the 'slurry'.

Despite all this, the sausage story is far from being one of gloom and doom. There is an increasing number of people making real sausages with real meat and without preservatives, colourings, phosphates (so they absorb water) and so on. One does, however, have to beware of the butcher who appears to be making his own 'special recipe' sausages. He may be just mincing up some meat, adding water and rusk and then tipping in a packet of mix containing herbs and spices, preservatives, colourings, flavourings and goodness only knows what else. Technically, the sausages are 'home-made' but unless the butcher is also a chemist, I would doubt that he has any idea of exactly what is in them.

By law, a pork sausage has to contain sixty-five per cent meat, although only half of this has to be lean meat. The remainder can be fat. The other thirty-five per cent is made up of spices, water and either bread or rusk. Bread was always the binder added to sausages in the past but is used very rarely these days. Rusk is easier, gives a more consistent result and, if you are wanting to produce a preservative-free sausage, extends the shelf-life. Micro-organisms in bread can quickly set up a reaction causing moulding in the sausage. Most high-quality sausages contain at least seventy per cent meat of which only a third is fat.

If you want to eat a really good sausage and, in my experience many people do, you have two alternatives. Find someone who makes the kind of sausage you like or make them yourself. When describing the different regional sausages in the next few pages, I have given the recipe if I know it and if I know or have been told of a good supplier, I have given their name. Their address, telephone number, hours of opening and various other pieces of information are all given at the end of the chapter relating to their region.

To Make Your Own Sausages

The first thing you need is some natural skins. If you are on good terms with your local butcher he may let you have some, otherwise they are available by mail order from Gysin & Hanson, W Weschenfelder & Sons and Small Holding Supplies. The easiest way to fill the sausages is by using the attachment Kenwood make for their mixers. Failing that you can either use a large piping bag fitted with a plain nozzle or, as a last resort, return to Queen Victoria's method with a funnel and push the mixture through by hand. Do not fill the casing too full or you will find that as the sausage cooks and expands it will burst. Always leave the sausages for at least one hour before cooking or, preferably, overnight.

Ingredients

A certain amount of fat is essential for the making of a good sausage in order to keep it moist, so although we all like our sausages leaner than our forefathers, do not be tempted to omit it completely. There are two kinds of fat generally used in sausage-making; the soft flair and belly fat and the hard back fat, the latter being used extensively in 100 per cent meat sausages.

The bread used in sausages needs to be a firm, old-fashioned type. The over-aerated sort cooked in steam ovens and sold in hot bread shops and in-store bakeries is not suitable. If it is a few days old, so much the better. In the old days, the bakers would always sell their stale loaves off to the butchers for sausage making — a mutually beneficial arrangement.

Quality herbs and spices are important for making good sausages. I always used to think that certain spice manufacturers just charged more for putting the same thing in fancy jars that others put in plastic. However, as with so many other things, there really is a difference between the higher and the lower grades. Freshness is also important. They lose their flavour after a few months so any that have been lurking in the back of the cupboard for a year or so should really be thrown out!

CAMBRIDGE SAUSAGE

Effectively, the Cambridge sausage is the standard British sausage flavoured with sage, thyme, cayenne, ground mace, nutmeg, pepper and salt. Among the best I have tried, (and I would emphasize that there must be literally hundreds of others that I have not had the opportunity of trying), are Nigel Schofield of Bangers's eighty per cent pork sausages and Emory St Marcus's English pork sausages. Both these suppliers also have a wide range of other sausages, as well as the standard ones including Algerian merguez, garlic etc. Heal's Farm in Devon also produce excellent sausages from their traditionally-reared meat but they are very expensive.

◆

175g/6 oz white bread, crusts removed
900g/2 lb lean pork
225g/8 oz pork fat
these can both come from a shoulder or hand joint
½ teaspoon dried sage
¼ teaspoon dried thyme
¼ teaspoon ground mace
¼ teaspoon grated nutmeg
¼ teaspoon freshly-milled white pepper
2 teaspoons salt

◆

Put the bread to soak in cold water for 10 minutes, then wring quite dry with your hands. Mince the lean and fat pork. Add the bread together with all the seasonings and mix well, then push into the skins.

Makes 1.35kg/3 lb

CUMBERLAND SAUSAGE

This is the only traditional 100 per cent meat sausage of the British Isles. Technically, it is not actually 100 per cent as two per cent of this is herbs and seasonings. It is also the only sausage which is not formed into links but left as one long sausage. I believe various reasons are given for this but the one I heard was that the Cumbrian houses have very low ceilings. It was, therefore, impractical to hang the sausages on hooks near the fire where they would be put to lightly smoke. A quick jump and presumably the sheep dog would have woofed the lot! Instead, they were supported by hooks horizontally across the chimney breast.

High quality Cumberland sausages can be found in many small butcher shops throughout the Lake District. Don't forget the golden rule and that is to actually ask the butcher what he puts into them and don't buy them if he won't tell you!

◆

900g/2 lb lean pork
450g/1 lb belly pork
225g/8 oz back fat
¼ teaspoon dried sage
¼ teaspoon dried rosemary
¼ teaspoon dried thyme
A good pinch cayenne pepper
¼ teaspoon grated nutmeg
½ teaspoon freshly-milled white pepper
2 teaspoons salt

◆

Mince the lean pork, belly pork and back fat. Add all the seasonings, mix well then use to fill the sausage skins.

Cumberland sausages can be put under a moderate grill and cooked slowly, turning them once. An even better way is to put them in a moderate oven, 180°C/350°F/Gas Mark 4 for 30–40 minutes or until golden brown.

Makes 1.8kg/4 lb

EPPING SAUSAGE

Twenty years ago I remember hearing about how wonderful the sausages from Epping were, doubtless due to the large herds of pigs the forest used to support. Unfortunately, little is heard of them these days.

GLOUCESTER SAUSAGE

This is similar to the Oxford sausage in that beef suet is added rather than pork fat. However the seasonings etc. are more like that of a Cambridge sausage and it is always put into skins.

LEICESTERSHIRE TOMATO SAUSAGE

One finds this sausage in many parts of the Midlands and up into Yorkshire. Ralph's of Melton Mowbray do a good one as does Philip Smith at Yorkshire's Oldest Pork Shop in Bradford.

Originally, I imagine either fresh tomato purée or concassé tomatoes (peeled, pips removed and finely chopped) were used. For convenience I suggest using concentrated, canned purée.

◆

175g/6 oz white bread, crusts removed
900g/2 lb lean pork
225g/8 oz pork fat
these can both come from a shoulder or hand joint
5 tablespoons tomato purée
1 teaspoon dried sage
¼ teaspoon ground mace
½ teaspoon grated nutmeg
½ teaspoon freshly-milled white pepper
2 teaspoons salt

◆

Make as the Cambridge sausage (page 27).

Makes 1.35kg/3 lb

LINCOLNSHIRE SAUSAGE

The Lincolnshire sausage is completely different from other sausages in that the only flavouring used, other than salt and pepper, is sage. This makes them a very vivid green. They are also best if left in a cool place to mature for 2–3 days before eating.

If you talk to any of the older Lincolnshire butchers, they will tell you that they never used to eat a Lincolnshire sausage until it was a week old and that it was at its best when it had whiskers growing from it! Quite why this did not give them all food poisoning I am not quite certain, but possibly the combination of the salt and sage effectively preserved them. It may also have been the same kind of reaction which occurs in the making of air-dried sausages, causing the white bloom on the outside.

The use of breadcrumbs may also have had something to do with it, as the traces of yeast remaining can also cause fermentation. This is why almost all sausage-makers these days use a yeastless bread rusk. It should also be remembered that very little pork was eaten in those months which did not have an 'r' in them and that applied to sausages as well. So, they would only have been made when the weather was comparatively cool.

Stamford is a good town in which to find traditional Lincolnshire sausages and Nelsons of Stamford produce some of the best. If you do not live within easy reach of Lincolnshire, this is a good sausage to make yourself at home. It is much simpler than others which depends upon minute adjustments to seasoning in order to achieve a really good result.

◆

175g/6 oz white bread, crusts removed
900g/2 lb lean pork
225g/8 oz pork fat
these can both come from a shoulder or hand joint
2 teaspoons dried sage
2 teaspoons salt
½ teaspoon freshly-milled white pepper

◆

Make as the Cambridge sausage (page 27).

Makes 1.35kg/3 lb

OXFORD SAUSAGE

These are unusual for a variety of reasons. Firstly, they are made with equal parts of lean pork and veal, together with beef suet. Old recipes suggest that this should be in the same proportion, but with our modern preference for less fatty food, I think the amount suggested below is plenty. Secondly, they always have the addition of grated lemon rind and thirdly, they are never put into skins.

◆

225g/8 oz lean pork
225g/8 oz lean veal
100g/4 oz beef suet
100g/4 oz fresh white breadcrumbs
Grated rind 1 small lemon
½ teaspoon dried sage
½ teaspoon dried thyme
½ teaspoon dried marjoram
Pinch of freshly-grated nutmeg
1 teaspoon salt
Freshly-milled black pepper
A little flour

◆

Mince the pork and veal together and put into a bowl. Coarsely grate the beef suet, if it is not already shredded, and add to the meats together with all the remaining ingredients, except the flour.

Mix together thoroughly with your hands then form into about 12 sausages. Toss lightly in a little flour. The sausages will hold their shape better if they are left overnight before cooking and this also helps the flavours to develop. Either fry in a little oil for about 15 minutes or put under a moderate grill.

Makes about 12 (or 675g/1½ lb) sausages

BLACK PUDDING

In the days when pigs were killed at home, it was always the job of the youngest member of the household to stir the pig's blood to prevent it from coagulating while the meat was being butchered. How young this youngest member would have been history does not seem to record, but presumably over seven or eight or the mess they would have got themselves into does not bear thinking about! Boring a job as it might have been, it was a very important one as once the blood had coagulated, it would not set again.

Black puddings were, and still are, made all over the British Isles but it is the north of England and the northern Midlands where the best traditions of black pudding making (and eating) remain intact. Every year, national black pudding championships are held and the winner is almost always a northerner. They have even been known to walk off with the prizes at the competition at Mortagne-au-Perche in France.

For most black pudding makers, the chief problem these days is obtaining the fresh blood, unless they are lucky enough to have a good abattoir nearby. The job of keeping the blood on the move to prevent coagulation is now done by machine, but even so, the black puddings really need to be made within a few hours of the pigs being killed. Many butchers have consequently had to resort to using dried haemoglobin which is readily available through the trade.

This would also be the easiest way of making them at home, but as I cannot envisage many people wanting to try, I have not given any recipes. Should your enthusiasm be such that you want to have a go, I would suggest reading Jane Grigson's *Charcuterie and French Pork Cookery* or Antony and Araminta Hippesley Coxe's *Book of Sausages*, both of which give several recipes.

Recipes vary considerably with virtually every butcher having his own secret 'mix'. The chief differences lie firstly in the seasonings used and secondly in the quantity and type of cereal added. French black puddings often contain no cereal at all, but in Britain some is almost always added. The amount increases when it comes to the cheaper, commercially-produced varieties. The cereals used are generally oatmeal, groats (whole oatmeal kernels) or barley, but rusk may be added as well.

The blood is mixed with the cereal, seasoning, possibly some finely-chopped onions, finely-chopped flair fat and/or hard back fat, poured into large casings made from the intestines and very gently boiled. It is extremely important that they are not boiled too quickly as the casings will burst with the inevitable disastrous results. Sometimes the mixture is simply baked in a tin without any casings and you will see large slabs of pudding for sale. Generally, I think the ones boiled in casings are more moist.

It may seem strange that something savoury like this is called a pudding when the word now refers to a sweet dish, but it was not until the pudding cloth was introduced in 1617 in Cambridge that the sweet pudding made its appearance. Prior to that, puddings were savoury dishes. Sometimes they were made with suet pastry but cooked, like a haggis, in the intestine of an animal. The use of the pudding cloth revolutionized the cooking of puddings, enabling sweet dishes to be cooked as well as savoury ones. The early sweet puddings were usually very simple, such as the Sussex Pond Pudding which merely had a lump of creamed butter and sugar in the middle of a ball of suet pastry.

Generally a black pudding is cut into slices and either fried or grilled to form an essential part of a northern breakfast or mixed grill. If preferred, small whole puddings can also be boiled and then cut into slices to serve. In British cookery it is not usual to add them to stews and casseroles, but you would be surprised at the difference a few well-flavoured slices can make.

PIES

There are few better forms of simple fare than a *freshly-baked* pork pie, whether it is home-made or comes from a small butcher who bakes them daily on the premises. Freshness is the key to a good pork pie to ensure that the pastry is really crisp. Refrigeration and covering with any form of plastic wrapping can cause the pastry to become slightly soggy. This is why, even if large commercial manufacturers use top quality meat, their products are never going to equal that of a small local butcher.

There are people who would disagree with this and feel that the flavour of the meat improves if it is left to mature for a couple of days. However even in a cool larder, covered with a simple gauze or muslin to keep off the flies, the pastry can lose some of its crispness after twenty-four hours.

Having now tasted more pork pies than I care to remember, there are two that stand out as being exceptional, and both were eaten slightly warm. One came from Edis of Ely in Cambridgeshire and the other from Weegman's in Otley, West Yorkshire.

MELTON MOWBRAY PIES

Melton Mowbray in Leicestershire is, of course, the town most celebrated for its pork pies. I was, however, just a little disappointed in the ones I bought there, having tasted better elsewhere. Dickinson and Morris are the last of the old manufacturers remaining and their attractive shop in Nottingham Road, where they also sell the famed Melton Hunt Cake, is certainly worth a visit, even if only to see the façade.

Whatever the merits of the pies currently being produced in Melton, the story behind their rise to fame is an interesting one. As the popularity and demand for Stilton cheese increased, so did the pig population of Leicestershire as the pigs were fed on the whey discarded during cheesemaking.

Baking and pork butchery are two industries which have often gone hand in hand, as baking is an excellent way of using up excess lard. Of all the pastries, hot water crust is one of the most difficult to handle and is best made by a professional. Indeed, at one time, bands of pastry makers used to travel from village to village during the autumn to prepare this pastry for the cottagers and farmers once they had slaughtered their stock.

In 1831, using his expertise as a baker and a cheap and plentiful supply of pork and lard, Edward Adcock, who owned a baker's and confectioner's in Leicester Street, Melton, started to make and bake pork pies. So successfeul was his enterprise that he was quickly imitated and by the middle of the 1870s there were a number of different manufacturers. An extract from a copy of The Daily Telegraph in 1877 shows the extent of their popularity. 'Is not Melton Mowbray celebrated from the Indus to the Pole for its raised pies and do not the firms of Collins & Co., Evans and Hill and Tebbut and Co. despatch thousands of these delicacies every day to all parts of the world by the morning passenger trains?'

How, though, had the word been spread in a mere forty years? The answer lies in a word – hunting. Foxhunting was at its zenith

of popularity in the mid-nineteenth century. The advent of the railways had made travelling easier and people came from all over England to hunt with packs like the Quorn and Belvoir. Pork pies became popular at hunt breakfasts and teas and they could also be cut into convenient portions, wrapped up and put into a pocket to provide a filling and nutritious snack during the day. When people returned home they frequently took pies with them, as did many of the grooms and hunt servants who only worked in Leicestershire during the hunting season.

The two distinctive differences still remaining between a Melton Mowbray pie and pork pies from other parts of England are firstly, that the Melton pie is always made with fresh pork which gives the filling a distinctive, grey appearance. Secondly, it is always hand-raised round a mould rather than being made in a tin.

Hand raising is a technique which, I am assured, is very easy once you get the knack of it. It is one I have not yet mastered successfully, other than for small pies. I find that either I take the pastry off the mould too early and it promptly collapses or, if I leave it a little longer so that it sets, it is impossible to remove from the mould without the pastry splitting and cracking.

Part of the problem may be my desire not to make the pastry too thick, plus the fact that if I am going to the bother of making one myself, I want a large one. As this is likely to be the case for most people, in the recipe below I have therefore abandoned the traditional method and baked the pie in a 15-cm/6-in loose-bottomed cake tin. Butchers and other pork pie specialists who do not hand-raise their pies generally use hoops, similar to deep crumpet rings, which they remove half way through cooking. This is the same principle.

Most recipes also suggest that, once the pie has been baked, it is filled with stock made from boiling pork bones with added herbs and vegetables. I find that this is not really necessary if you are going to eat the pie within a day or two as the pork itself generates enough juices to keep it moist, which set into a gel once the pie has cooled.

◆

350g/12 oz hot water crust pastry (page 142)
900g/2 lb coarsely-minced lean pork (see note)
2 teaspoons salt
Freshly-milled black pepper
1 tablespoon chopped fresh sage or 1 teaspoon dried sage
Beaten egg for glazing

NOTE: The proportion should be approximately two-thirds lean meat to one-third fat. You can make it three-quarters to one-quarter if you prefer but a certain amount of fat is essential to keep it moist.

◆

Grease a 15-cm/6-in loose-bottomed cake tin with lard, then lightly dust with flour. Knead the pastry thoroughly until it is smooth. Cut off a quarter of it, wrap it in clingfilm and put on one side. Put the remaining pastry into the tin and, using your fingers, gently mould it round the inside until it comes about 1.25cm/½ in above the rim of the tin. Try to make the pastry as even as possible and make certain there are no holes in it. Put on one side while preparing the filling.

Mix the pork with the seasoning and sage, kneading the mixture well with your hands so that they are evenly mixed in. You can add a few spices if you wish, such as nutmeg or mace, but this is not traditional for a Melton Mowbray pie.

Carefully pack the meat into the pastry case, then brush the edges with beaten egg. Roll out the remaining pastry to a circle for the lid. Place in position, trim the edges then mark them with a fork to decorate them. Make a large hole in the centre for the steam to escape. Any pastry trimmings can then be rolled out and cut into leaves to decorate the top. Lightly brush these with beaten egg and place in position.

Bake in a hot oven, 220°C/425°F/Gas Mark 7 for 15 minutes. Reduce the heat to 180°C/350°F/Gas Mark 4 and bake for a further 45 minutes. Remove the pie from the oven and, very gently, push up the base of the tin to remove the pie, using a pair of oven gloves. Care must be taken during this operation, firstly that you do not burn yourself with the sides of the cake tin, and also that you do not break or crack the pastry. Brush all over the pastry with beaten egg, making sure that the hole in the top is not sealed up. If the steam is unable to escape at the top, it is liable to burst the sides open which will result in all the meat juices being lost.

Replace in the oven for a further 30 minutes or until golden brown. Remove from the oven and allow to cool, then serve either warm or cold with plenty of mustard.

Serves 8–10

MARKET HARBOROUGH PIE

Neighbouring Market Harborough produces a pork pie which has the same basis as the Melton Mowbray pie but it also contains sliced apples and onions. This adds moisture as well as flavour and makes an altogether more interesting pie. Its origins are more closely linked to the earliest pork pies as a fourteenth-century recipe instructs that you should 'lay in your coffyn a good store of raisins and currants' before adding the meat.

◆

350g/12 oz hot water crust pastry (page 142)
675g/1½ lb coarsely-minced pork
1½ teaspoons salt
Freshly-milled black pepper
1 tablespoon chopped fresh sage or 1 teaspoon dried sage
1 large cooking apple, peeled and thinly sliced
1 medium-sized onion, peeled and thinly sliced
1 tablespoon sugar

◆

Follow the instructions for the Melton Mowbray pie, adding the seasoning and sage to the pork. Pack half the meat into the pastry, cover with the apple, then the onion and sprinkle with the sugar. Gently pack the remaining meat on top then continue and bake as the Melton Mowbray pie.

Serves 8–10

YORKSHIRE PORK PIE

In Yorkshire they like their pork pies to have a pinkish tinge to the meat, rather than the grey of the Midlands pies. This is generally achieved by lightly pickling the pork for a couple of days. Philip Smith, who owns and runs Yorkshire's Oldest Pork Shop in Ivegate, Bradford, told me that he feels an easier way for the housewife to achieve this is by using a mixture of fresh pork and bacon. This is what he recommends when he gives demonstrations.

His shop, in which trading started as far back as 1714, is a fascinating emporium. He not only makes all his own pies, sausages and black puddings (indeed he won the title of Champion Black Pudding Maker in 1977), he also sells a wide range of freshly-roasted pork joints including rolled shoulder, belly, cheeks and shanks. His other speciality, which I found nowhere else, is freshly-boiled pig's parts which include tails, trotters, ears and snouts, the latter being considered a great delicacy.

Yorkshire hot water crust is also slightly different in that it is usual to add an egg yolk which enriches it. I think this is an improvement on the basic recipe.

◆

350g/12 oz hot water crust pastry (page 142) plus 1 egg yolk (see below)
675g/1½ lb pork shoulder meat
225g/8 oz lean, unsmoked streaky bacon
½ teaspoon grated nutmeg
1 teaspoon dry English mustard
Salt and freshly-milled black pepper

◆

Make the pastry following the basic method on page 142 but once the flour has been sieved into the bowl, make a well in the centre and add the egg yolk. Sprinkle this with a layer of flour about 1.25-cm/½-in thick, then pour the hot lard and water on top and continue in the normal way.

Mince the pork and bacon, mix thoroughly together, then add the nutmeg, mustard and seasoning and mix well. Follow the recipe for the Melton Mowbray pie.

Serves 8–10

BRAWN

The Oxford dictionary's definition of *brawn* is muscle and lean flesh and from it comes *brawny*, meaning muscular strength. In her excellent book *The Cookery of England*, Elizabeth Ayrton points out that in middle English the word *brawn* (also spelt *brawne* and *braune*) simply meant meat. More often than not this was the leg of a boar, but sometimes it was mutton, pork and even capon.

This explains some of the strange sounding directions found in old books which instruct one to soak 'brawn' after cooking in brine to which ale or wine and spices had been added. An excellent method of preservation as well as a way of adding flavour to meat, it was used particularly for the extremities of the pig, such as the head and trotters.

It is not known if in Russell's statement in his *Book of Nurture* published in 1460, 'Set forth mustard and brawne' he actually meant meat or a brawn. Certainly brawns as we know them today, i.e. meat usually from the head of a pig firmly set in jellied stock, were extremely popular medieval dishes and were always served with mustard sauce. These brawns were direct descendants of Norman savoury jellies in which both fish and meat were put to set in a jelly that had been highly coloured with saffron.

Medieval brawns were elaborate dishes generally served at banquets and during the twelve days of feasting over Christmas. They were frequently moulded and castellated, decorated with piped cream and gilded with gold leaf. So large were these set pieces that they were often referred to as a 'shield of brawn'.

Over the centuries, brawn gradually developed into more humble fare. This status perhaps best being illustrated by the way it was sometimes referred to as *head cheese*, which corresponded to beef cheese, i.e. a fairly simple meat loaf. It did, however, enjoy a revival during the nineteenth century as the Victorians took any opportunity they could to mould and decorate food. Brawn was a natural for this treatment.

Today it seems to be enjoyed mainly by the older generations. In the pork butcher shops I have visited where they have pots of home-made brawn, one rarely sees young people buying it. No doubt this is largely because they have been brought up on pâté which they consider to be superior. Much factory-produced pâté is excellent but some of the cheaper varieties leave a good deal to be desired and a proper well-made brawn would be preferable.

If you enjoy a good home-made brawn, the recipe below is well worth trying.

LINCOLNSHIRE BRAWN

◆

½ pig's head
2 pig's trotters
½ nutmeg
20 black peppercorns
10 cloves
3 bay leaves
2 blades mace
1 tablespoon dried sage
1 bunch parsley
1 teaspoon salt
Water

◆

Remove the brains and the eyeball from the head if this has not already been done. Wash the head thoroughly in cold water. Split the trotters in half. Grate the nutmeg, but if you have two or three small pieces which are too small to grate they can be just added whole. Put all the ingredients into a large pan. Cover with cold water and bring to the boil. Remove any scum from the surface, cover the pan and simmer *very gently* for about 4 hours or until the meat is very tender. If preferred, the pan can be put into a low oven.

Allow the meat and liquor to cool for about an hour, then strain the meat, reserving the liquor. Take the meat off the bones, discarding all the skin, gristle, excess fat, etc. Chop the meat finely and put it into a 1.2-litre/2-pt bowl. While doing this, boil 600 ml/1 pt of the stock rapidly until it is reduced by half. Taste and add a little extra salt if necessary. It is important not to add too much salt at first or on reduction the stock can become over salty. Strain over the meat, then leave overnight to set in a cool place.

To turn out, quickly dip the basin into a bowl of very hot water, then invert on to a serving plate. Serve with crusty bread and salad.

Serves 6–8

FAGGOTS

Looking through books for pork recipes, I think I came across more recipes for faggots (also known as Savoury Ducks or Poor Man's Goose) than for anything else. Some said they were a speciality of Wiltshire, some said Wales, others said the north of England, and still others said East Anglia! From all this one can safely assume that faggots are made throughout the British Isles. Some recipes may claim to be a speciality of a region (and recipes do vary considerably), but the chances are that a similar one is being made 200 miles away! They have certainly been around a long time though, because as Antony and Araminta Hippisley-Coxe point out in their *Book of Sausages*, it was a batch of faggots cooking in a baker's shop in Pudding Lane which started the Great Fire of London in 1666.

On my travels around the British Isles, I have tasted countless faggots prepared by butchers on the premises. Some were quite delicious, others positively disgusting and over-cooked and many with a tendency to be dry. The reason for the latter is that they were cooked without the thin veil of pork caul fat which is essential for the making of a good faggot.

This is becoming increasingly difficult to obtain as more butchers buy their meat ready-jointed and even some specialist pork butchers do not sell it. However, if you are determined to make faggots, it can be obtained direct from an abattoir if it is ordered in advance.

Originally faggots were made with the pluck of the pig which includes the liver, heart, lungs and spleen. However, as pluck, like caul, becomes increasingly difficult to obtain, more faggots are being made with just the liver and some fresh pork. The two recipes below are very different in the way they are made, so it is worth trying both and seeing which one you prefer, but the pluck and liver are interchangeable.

FAGGOTS 1

◆

A piece of pig's caul
450g/1 lb pig's pluck (see opposite)
225g/8 oz fat pork belly
2 large onions
100g/4 oz fresh white breadcrumbs
¼ teaspoon ground mace
1 tablespoon chopped fresh sage or 1 teaspoon dried sage
Salt and freshly-milled black pepper
300 ml/½ pt stock

◆

Put the caul to soak in tepid water while preparing the mixture. Either mince the pluck, pork belly and onions together or put into a blender or food processor and process until fairly smooth. Add the breadcrumbs, mace, sage and seasoning and mix well.

Lay out the caul on a working surface and cut into 12 squares approximately 10cm/4 in. Form the minced meat into 12 balls and wrap each one in a piece of caul fat. Place close together in a baking dish. Pour over the stock. Bake in a moderate oven, 180°C/350°F/ Gas Mark 4 for about 1 hour or until browned. Serve hot with mashed potatoes and vegetables, but peas are especially good.

Serves 6

FAGGOTS 2

◆

A piece of pig's caul
450g/1 lb pig's liver
350g/12 oz fat pork belly
2 medium-sized onions, finely chopped
15g/½ oz butter
Salt and freshly-milled black pepper
¼ teaspoon grated nutmeg
1 tablespoon chopped fresh sage or 1 teaspoon dried sage
2 teaspoons chopped fresh thyme or ½ teaspoon dried thyme
175g/6 oz fresh white breadcrumbs
2 eggs, beaten

◆

Put the caul to soak in tepid water. Either mince the liver and belly pork and onions or put into a blender or food processor and process until fairly smooth. Melt the butter in a pan, add the meat and onions together with the salt and pepper, nutmeg, sage and thyme. Cover and cook gently over a low heat for 30 minutes. Remove from the heat, allow to cook for 10 minutes, then add the breadcrumbs and eggs. Taste and adjust the seasoning.

Lay out the caul on a working surface and cut into 12 squares approximately 10cm/4 in. Form the minced meat into 12 balls and wrap each one in a piece of caul fat. Place close together in a baking dish.

Bake in a moderately hot oven, 190°C/375°F/Gas Mark 5 for 30 minutes or until browned. Remove and serve hot as for the previous recipe or allow to cool and serve cold with salad.

Serves 6

BACON AND HAM

At one time very little of the pig was eaten fresh, other than the offal and possibly the shoulder and hand. The leg would have been cut off and cured separately for ham, whilst the remainder of the side or flitch, as it was generally called, would have been dry-salted or brined and then left to dry to make bacon.

Bacon was, in fact, the mainstay of the larder for most country dwellers. In his *Cottage Economy* published in 1822, William Cobbett extolled the virtues of bacon in the following manner: 'Other meat you may have, but bacon is the great thing. It is always ready; as good cold as hot; goes to the field or the coppice conveniently; in harvest and other busy times, demands the pot to be boiled only on Sunday; has twice as much strength in it as any other thing of the same weight; and, in short has in it every quality that tends to make a labourer's family able to work and be well off.'

There are two ways in which bacon is produced. Dry-salting was the popular old country method, and curing in brine is the method most commonly used today. Both have their disciples, but it would be true to say that modern methods of brine-curing enable the production of less heavily-salted bacon, which is more acceptable for modern palates. Refrigeration has also played a vital role in this as it is no longer necessary to cure bacon so that it will keep for months or, as was common practice, years. Once the bacon had been cured, the entire flitch was frequently either buried in wood ash to keep off the flies and the insects, or it would be wrapped in muslin and given several coats of whitewash. This made it impervious, not only to insects but also to damp.

It was the Romans who first differentiated between bacon and ham. Ham (*perna*) was prepared quite differently from shoulder bacon (*petaso*) according to Apicius. Both were boiled with figs, but ham was baked in a flour and oil paste (similar to a huff paste) and bacon was browned and served with a wine and pepper sauce.

Confusion sometimes exists over the differences between bacon, gammon and ham, but really it is quite simple. Bacon is any part of the pig excluding the leg, which is either dry-salted or cured in a wet brine and then left to dry and mature. Once matured, which can take from seven to eleven days, it can be eaten as unsmoked or green bacon, or it can then be smoked, which many people feel improves the flavour and extends its keeping qualities.

The hind leg or ham of the pig, as it was known even on the live animal, was always cut off and cured separately. The main reason for this being that as a large joint, it took considerably longer for the salt to penetrate through to the bone and cure it than for the remainder of the carcass. At one time 30 and 40 lb hams were common, and some weighed as much as 60 lb.

More modern methods of curing, largely introduced by the Harris Bacon Company at the end of the last century (page 56), and the fact that pigs are smaller, means that it is now possible to cure the leg with the remainder of the side. This is gammon.

Ham is generally considered to be superior to gammon. However, there really should be no difference between a gammon and a ham if they are cured the same way and, indeed, many hams that are sold, especially the cooked variety, are technically gammons. The superiority lies in the fact that many hams are salted, cured with herbs and spices, possibly smoked and left to mature in old traditional ways which improves the flavour. These processes involve time, money and expertise which is why the majority of hams are more expensive than gammon and are less easily obtainable.

Pigs that are to be used for bacon are usually slaughtered when they are about six months old and weigh between 57kg and 75kg/ 125 lb and 165 lb. Those sold for fresh pork are only about four months old and weigh 55kg–60kg/121 lb–135 lb. Sometimes even larger pigs are used, in which case some of the fat and rind is removed prior to curing. Despite our desire for lean meat, a certain amount of fat is essential for successful bacon curing. This is even more true of ham curing and many of the people using traditional dry-cures and methods bemoan the fact that they are unable to obtain legs with sufficient fat on them.

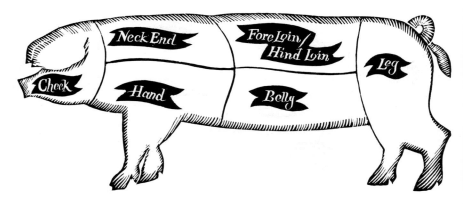

CURING BACON

We used to own a cottage in Pembrokeshire and our neighbour, Mrs Davies (what else would she be called?) still farmed in a timeless fashion. Her chickens ran not only all over her farmyard, but in the adjacent road. Indeed her highest cause of mortality amongst them was not Mr Fox, but cars. She had no refrigerator but kept a pig in the garden and cured her own bacon, which hung from the beams of the kitchen above the range. As a special concession, as she did not usually sell, she let me have some one day. I remember it clearly for its fattiness and its saltiness.

This first tasting of dry-salted, home-cured bacon has been borne out by others I have tried from butchers throughout the country. My father, who is in his seventies, thinks this kind of bacon is marvellous, but it appears that it is only his generation who is continuing to buy it. The post war bunch, like myself, prefer a milder cure, which is generally achieved by curing in a brine.

By brine, I mean a mixture of only salt, water, a few herbs and spices, saltpetre (sodium or potassium nitrate) possibly some sal prunella (sodium or potassium nitrite) and sugar, but certainly no phosphates. Phosphates are added simply because they enable the meat to absorb water, so that it is heavier and fetches a higher price.

Salt is the best preserving agent in the world and is really the only ingredient that is essential for making either bacon or ham. Saltpetre is added for a variety of reasons. It is an oxidizing agent which kills the decomposing bacteria. During this process some of the nitrates become nitrites. These speed up the action of the salt, as well as imparting the attractive pink colour which marks all

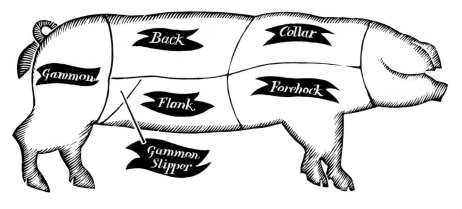

salted meats. In the old days when a brine and the equipment were used over and over again, these nitrites became very highly developed but it is now possible to add them in the form of sal prunella. These two products now have E numbers, saltpetre being E252 and sal prunella E251, and this has caused unnecessary concern amongst some sections of the public. However, there is possibly a little justification about the usage of any *excess* sal prunella. It should be remembered that they are both naturally occurring substances which have been used for centuries without any known serious detrimental effects. The quantities used are minute and are considered by all the experts not to constitute any kind of health hazard, unless cured meats are eaten almost to the total exclusion of all other foods.

The salt used for any kind of curing should never be free-running table salt as this has a non-caking agent added to it. Good quality rock salt or natural sea salt are the two best kinds to use. Old fashioned cookery books frequently refer to the use of bay salt, an old word for rock salt. Once the brine has been made, it is important that it is allowed to become quite cold before the meat is added. If it is warm, especially in warm weather, instead of preserving the meat it can putrify it.

In her *Food in England,* Dorothy Hartley points out that a 'curious old belief . . . that no woman at her monthly period, nor any woman just recovered from childbed, should handle any form of salting. This is firm belief in many farms, and they will go to much trouble and expense to bring another hand to carry on the work if the mother of the house cannot. Some of the old women workers may have fostered the belief in order to make themselves indispensable to the younger women – but some put it down to the woman having a slight temperature at the time, as all such work should have a *cool* hand.'

I had often wondered why pork is the meat most commonly salted, and have only recently discovered the answer. Pork requires less salt for curing than other meat, an important aspect in the past when salt was a scarce commodity and was even subject to a tax.

Salt also has a drying effect on meat. The more used, the drier and tougher the meat becomes, so that lamb and beef become almost inedible. Bacon is not immune from this problem and much that was cured in Saxon times undoubtedly suffered, hence the derogatory term *chaw-bacon*. This drying can be counteracted by the addition of sugar and honey and lead directly to the production of sweet-cures. You will find, though, that a small amount of sugar is always added to brines and dry-cures as a preventive measure.

ALL-PURPOSE BRINE

This brine can be used to produce pickled pork and bacon. Pickled pork, which is not seen nearly as frequently these days, is really the first stage of bacon production. The pieces of pork are left in the brine for anything from three days, for mild-cured small joints weighing 900g/2 lb, to up to ten days for a whole shoulder or leg, again mild-cured. They can be left longer than this, in which case the salt level should be checked and additional salt, dissolved in water, added if it has become low. Professional meat curers use a brineometer, but for the home curer, taste is as good an indication as any.

When pork has only been given a mild cure for a few days, it does not require soaking or pre-boiling, but if it has been left in the brine for a while, it is advisable to soak it for several hours before using. If you wish to make bacon, leave it in the brine for a week for small pieces of back or streaky, weighing 1.25–1.8 kg/3–4 lb, but allow ten days or more for larger joints. Hang the piece of meat up to dry for a couple of days to remove all the moisture, then wrap in muslin and leave in a cool place to mature for at least a week. This wet-cured bacon does not keep as long as the dry-salted variety, so I would not advise keeping it for longer than a couple of months, and it should be refrigerated. It is important that both the brining and the maturing are carried out in a cool place. Refrigeration allows commercial bacon producers to carry on throughout the year, but in the home it was, and still is, an autumn and winter occupation. Beatrix Potter makes mention of this in her *Tale of Pigling Bland*. 'After supper Mr Piperson consulted an almanac, and felt Pigling's ribs, it was too late in the season for curing bacon. . . . He looked at the small remains of a flitch. . .'.

When brining meat, it is important that it does not come into contact with any form of metal. Old stone or earthenware crocks were used originally, or wooden tubs for dry-salting. If you are lucky enough to possess such a crock today, you are more likely to want to flaunt it filled with dried flowers than to actually use it for its original purpose. The most convenient thing to use is a new, or certainly very clean, plastic washing-up bowl, bucket or dustbin.

certainly very clean, plastic washing-up bowl, bucket or dustbin.

To ensure the meat stays submerged in the brine and does not rise to the surface, a piece of wooden board just a little smaller than the container needs to be placed on top of the meat and pressed down with a weight. Again, this cannot be made of metal, so some form of heavy jar is really the most convenient object, or a spare earthenware casserole filled with some of the brine.

◆

4.8 l./1 gal water
550g/1 lb 4 oz sea salt or good quality rock salt
550g/1 lb 4 oz sugar
2 tablespoons saltpetre
2 teaspoons juniper berries
½ nutmeg
1 teaspoon cloves
1 teaspoon black peppercorns
1 large sprig rosemary
3 bay leaves

◆

Put the water, salt, sugar and saltpetre into a large pan. Put all the remaining ingredients into a small square of muslin, tie it up and add to the pan. Bring the brine slowly to the boil, boil for 3 minutes then remove any scum and allow it to become *quite cold*. Strain into the bowl or bucket. Prick the meat all over with a carving fork as this helps the brine to penetrate evenly. Put into the brine then place a weighted board on top.

SMOKING

In the days when most people had kitchen ranges or large inglenook fireplaces in which the fires were kept going twenty-four hours a day, home-smoking presented very few problems. The ham, side of bacon or even sausages could happily be left up the chimney. Hams could sometimes be left for as long as six weeks as the smoke was not as concentrated as in a special smoking unit.

Home-cured bacon and ham do not need to be smoked, and it is quite a difficult business to do yourself, but if you are really enthusiastic you might like to try. To start with, I would recommend that you use a small, inexpensive joint of meat, such as a piece of streaky bacon, so that if the end result is slightly disappointing you have not wasted too much money.

The small home smokers which some people have are not suitable for bacon and ham as they hot-smoke, rather than cold-smoke the food and so, effectively, cook it. Oak and beech sawdust are the best to use and for a description of how to do it in an old beer barrel, one really cannot do better than Mrs Beeton.

'Take an old hogshead, stop all the crevices, and fix a place to put a cross-stick near the bottom, to hang the articles to be smoked on. Next, in the side, cut a hole near the top, to introduce an iron pan filled with sawdust, and small pieces of green wood. Having turned the tub upside down, hang the articles upon the cross-stick, introduce the iron pan in the opening, place a piece of red-hot iron in the pan, cover with sawdust, and all will be complete. Let a large ham remain for forty-eight hours and keep up a good smoke.'

SOAKING BACON AND HAM

For most of the commercially-produced bacon and ham which have a comparatively mild cure, soaking is no longer considered essential. All that is necessary is to put the joint into a pan of cold water, bring it *slowly* to the boil, discard this water and then cover it with fresh cold water.

I think this method works well for small joints under 1.2kg/3 lb, but anything over this I feel is better left to soak for about four hours. Nothing is more disappointing than cooking a beautiful-looking piece of meat and finding it is too salty. If baking any joint, even a small piece of forehock or gammon, I also think it is better to soak it.

When it comes to individually produced ham, do take advice from the curer as soaking times vary. Marsh York hams no longer have as much salt used in the curing as they used to, but a locally-cured farm ham could well need as long as seventy-two hours. This is the time recommended by Gerald Millhouse in Bristol for his Bradenham hams. Whole and half hams are not cheap purchases, so it is worth getting this simple initial stage right or the trouble and care taken, both in its production and in cooking, will be wasted.

COOKING BACON, GAMMON AND HAM

There are two basic ways in which bacon joints, gammon and ham are cooked besides baking and boiling, but there can be slight variations on these. Sometimes even a combination of the two methods are used and the meat is first boiled, which keeps it moist and succulent, and then baked in the oven to crisp the fat and give an attractive glaze. Whichever method of cooking is chosen, you want to allow 25 minutes per 450g/1 lb and 25 minutes over.

BOILING

This is the simplest method of cooking, but it is essential that the meat is not really *boiled* but simmered very *gently*. If you do boil the meat, you will find that you are left with something that is about half the size you started with.

Salt should not be added to the water which is usually flavoured with a few peppercorns, a bay leaf, a couple of peeled and quartered onions and a couple of peeled and roughly-chopped carrots. Some people also like to add a tablespoon or so of brown sugar.

As well as cooking in just water, the meat can be cooked in a mixture of ale and water, a mixture of cider and water, or simply cider on its own, or apple juice and water. Other flavourings which can be added include peeled orange rind and juice, cloves, allspice and ginger.

Another method of cooking which was recommended to me by a couple of people especially for brine-cured bacon and hams, is 'boil

in the bag'. Put the meat into a large roastabag or a heavy-duty polythene bag, together with any spices and seasonings you might like. Tie the bag loosely at the top and then put the bag into a pan of gently simmering water. When the meat is cooked, remove it from the pan, allow it to cool in the juices which have collected round it in the bag, then remove it when it is quite cold.

BAKING

In order that the meat does not dry out during cooking, if baking in the oven, it is essential that it is covered for at least half the cooking time (three-quarters if it is a whole ham). The usual way to do this these days is by covering with foil, but previously it was achieved by wrapping the meat in a huff crust.

I have tried this and found it successful for dry-cured hams, but not for brine-cured meats as too much water comes out of these. All you have to do is make a stiff flour and water paste. If it is too soft it will tend to collapse and split during cooking. Wrap it round the meat so that it is completely enveloped. I find that it takes longer for the heat to penetrate through the huff paste than foil, so it is better to allow 30 minutes per 450g/1 lb and 30 minutes over.

The usual temperature for the initial baking, whether in foil or a huff crust, is a moderate oven, 180°C/350°F/Gas Mark 4. If the meat is almost fully cooked and is being put into the oven purely to glaze it, a hot oven is preferable, i.e. 220°C/425°F/Gas Mark 7.

Whether the meat is wrapped in foil or a huff crust, you can still add seasonings of your choice to the 'parcel' before it is wrapped up, such as onions, bay leaves, cloves, honey, etc. If baking a whole ham in foil in the oven, it can be a good idea to completely wrap the joint in foil and put it in the roasting tin with 5cm/2 in of water which just helps to keep it moist.

GLAZES

Various glazes are spread over bacon, gammon joints and ham especially over the fat once the rind has been peeled off, so that it browns and crisps. Frequently, the fat is scored into diamonds and each diamond is studded with a clove.

MUSTARD AND BROWN SUGAR

This is the commonest and easiest glaze of all. One method is to spread the fat with a little made mustard then press a layer of demerara sugar about 0.75-cm/¼-in thick over the top and then bake in a hot oven until the fat is brown. Equally delicious is to mix 50g/2 oz soft brown sugar with 1 tablespoon dry English mustard and just spread this over the fat.

OXFORD GLAZE

Mix together 4 tablespoons Oxford marmalade and 2 tablespoons of demerara sugar and spread this thickly all over the meat. This is enough for a small joint weighing about 1.2kg/3 lb.

HONEY

Honey can be used just on its own or is excellent if a rounded teaspoon of mild English grain mustard is mixed with every tablespoon of honey. This mixture can then be spread all over the fat and the lean of the joint. For a spicier glaze, a little Worcestershire sauce can also be added.

CHAPTER FOUR
THE WEST COUNTRY
◆

There would appear to be more regional recipes in this part of England than any other. Whether this is because being rather cut off from the remainder of the country they have endured longer, or that the local people wrote them down so that they have been preserved, I do not know. It could even be that both the countryside and the food so inspired visiting writers that they recorded the recipes. It would certainly not be difficult to devote an entire book to West Country food of all kinds.

During the beginning of the nineteenth century when so many new breeds of pig were coming into being, there was both a Devon pig and a Cornish pig. Both these would appear to have descended from the Old English pig. Today the breed most closely related to this pig is the British Lop pig, a rather wonderfully old-fashioned looking animal which is still only found in the West Country and in very small numbers.

Of all the counties in England, Wiltshire is the one most closely associated with bacon and ham and this is almost entirely due to the Harris Bacon Company. In 1770 John Harris, together with his mother, opened a pork butcher's cum grocer's cum bakery in the village of Calne. Gradually their business expanded so that by the middle of the nineteenth century they were not only supplying the surrounding towns and villages with bacon but they were despatching to London as well. The family were extremely fortunate in that, by this time, a flourishing trade had developed in Irish pigs. They were shipped over to Wales and then slowly herded to London. One of their resting stops on the way was Calne which enabled the Harris's to buy up plenty of pork at a very reasonable price.

The potato famine in Ireland in 1847 put a stop to this trade, so a great-grandson of the original John Harris was sent to America to look at the possibility of importing pigs from there. He found this to be totally impractical, but came back from the States with the knowledge of how to build an ice house so that curing could be carried out throughout the year instead of only in the winter months.

Having overcome a few initial difficulties, in 1864 he took out a patent on the invention of 'An Improved Method of Constructing Rooms or Places for Curing and Preserving Meat or Perishable Articles'. This development transformed commercial bacon production as not only could bacon be cured throughout the year, but far less salt was needed to cure it in the first place.

It was at this time that Harris also took over production of the Bradenham ham which had been created by Lord Bradenham in 1781 and is considered by many to be the finest British ham. With its coal black skin and the emblem of a rearing winged horse or Pegasus stamped on to it, it is instantly recognizable. Production by Harris ceased completely during the 1970s but in 1983 production started again at their factory at Leeming Bar.

Having read about Gerald Millhouse of Bristol in Jane Grigson's *Observer Guide to British Cookery*, and in a cutting from a magazine article given to me by a friend, I went to see him on my way to Exmoor.

At Christmas he cures his own York and Bradenham hams and also, throughout the year, cures and smokes his own bacon. The smoking is done over beech sawdust which he buys from the local coffin maker as it is one of the few sources of unadulterated wood. In addition to his bacon, he also sells the *most delicious* cold-smoked pork loin chops and his 100 per cent meat pork and marjoram sausages are some of the best I have ever eaten.

Ben Watson of Riverford Farm Foods, Totnes in Devon rears his own pork, free from hormones and growth promoters and then cures it in a traditional brine-cure. The exact length of time the bacon is left in the cure depends on the fatness of the carcass and whether it is a boar or a gilt (female) pig as the boars require longer. The fatter they are the longer they take, which explains why brine-cures were not popular in the nineteenth century as the lean became 'water-logged'. Ten days is about the average time before removing it and leaving it to dry. Some is sold as unsmoked (green) bacon while the remainder is smoked. He also produces very good, thinly-sliced smoked pork loin in vacuum packs.

Additive-free pork is also available from the Real Meat Company in Wiltshire who have their own shop in Bath. They act as wholesaler to a number of butchers, whose names you can obtain from them on request. While generally kept in during the winter months, their pigs are allowed a fairly free-range lifestyle, but when housed are allowed plenty of space and fresh air. Also, the sows are not kept in stalls as they are on most intensive farms.

Devon Foods 15 Gandy Street, Exeter EX4 3LS
Tel: (0392) 221525 Open 9.30–5.30 Monday to Saturday.

Barnstaple Market (page 59) Pannier Market,
High Street. Open Tuesday and Friday.

Heal Farm Quality Traditional Meats
Kings Nympton, Umberleigh, Devon EX37 9TB
Tel: (07695) 2077. Open 9–5 Monday to Friday,
10–4 Saturday. Also mail order.

Real Meat Company (page 57) East Hill Farm,
Heytesbury, Wilts BA2 3QW
and 7 Hays Place, Bearfleet, Bath
Tel: (0225) 335139
Open 8–1 Monday, 8–5.30 Tuesday to Friday, 8–4 Saturday.

Ben Watson (page 57) Riverford Farm, Staverton, Totnes,
Devon TQ9 6AF Tel: (080 426) 523 Mail order.

Harris – Leeming Bar (page 56) Leeming Bar,
Northallerton, Yorkshire DL7 9AW Tel: (0677) 22661
Telephone orders and mail order.

Gerald Millhouse (page 57) The Mall, Clifton,
Bristol BS8 4DR Tel: (0272) 734440
Open 8–5.30 Monday to Friday, 8–5 Saturday.

Bangers Unit 4B, Lapford Cross Industrial
Estate, Lapford, Devon EX17 Tel: (03635) 794
Open 9–3 Monday to Thursday, 9–1 Friday and Saturday.

BATH CHAPS

Bath chaps, the cured cheek of the pig which is cooked and rolled in breadcrumbs can now be found in every corner of the British Isles. So popular at late ball suppers, when the Spa was in its heyday, they were produced from the local Gloucester Old Spot or the Old Gloucester as it probably was then.

These pigs have a peculiarly long jaw, which means that there is considerably more meat on them than on the modern large white pigs. The proportion of fat to lean in a Bath chap is very high, which has slightly decreased their popularity over the last few years. They do, however, make a very good lunch or supper when served in the traditional way with crusty bread, mustard or pickle.

Unless you happen to have a brine bath in operation or find yourself with half a pig's head, making Bath chaps at home is scarcely worthwhile. Home-cured, ready-cooked Bath chaps can be bought from any pork butcher.

Should your enthusiasm stretch that far, first immerse the chap together with the half tongue into a brine bath (page 49) for five to seven days. Remove from the brine, wrap in a piece of muslin, put into a pan of cold water and bring to the boil.

Discard the water, cover with fresh cold water and add a chopped onion or leek, a sprig of parsley and, if liked, a tablespoon of sugar. Boil gently for about 3 hours or until it is very tender. Allow it to cool for about 1 hour, then untie the muslin, take out all the bones and skin the chap.

Lay it between two boards with a weight on top to press it during cooling, then coat completely in toasted breadcrumbs.

HOG'S PUDDING

A speciality of Devon and Cornwall, hog's pudding is particularly popular in the north of Devon, around Barnstaple, where home-made hog's puddings can be found well displayed in every butcher's shop. Until recently, there was also an old boy who used to sell it on a stall at one of my favourite shopping haunts, Barnstaple market. He has now given up but you can still sometimes find a few farm-produced ones at some of the little stalls selling vegetables, if they happen to have recently killed a pig at home.

Basically hog's pudding is a sausage containing between seventy and eighty per cent meat, together with groats (whole kernels of oatmeal), spices and seasoning. It is stuffed into large intestines, like black pudding, to provide a natural casing. The pudding is then boiled, so it is effectively cooked when bought. Although it can be eaten cold, it is almost always served hot, either grilled or fried, cut in slices or cooked whole. It can then form a main meal with creamed potatoes and other vegetables but a few slices are an essential ingredient of a true West Country breakfast.

SOMERSET PORK CHOPS

The scrumpy, or home-made cider found in pubs or on the farms in the West Country bears little resemblance to the fizzy stuff bought in bottles. Hardly suprisingly, it varies considerably depending on the kind of apple grown, the soil in which it grows and, above all, the person pressing the cider. Generally though, it is dry, sometimes almost still, with a strong flavour which makes it ideal for cooking as well as drinking.

The affinity between pork and apples is legendary. Pork with apple sauce is the most obvious example, but there are countless others. Bacon and ham are often cooked or cured in cider and whatever shape or form the pork appears in, there is frequently apple not far away! If at all possible, this dish should be cooked with scrumpy, but failing that use ordinary bottled dry cider. Even then, you will find that it is a very easy way of transforming some very simple ingredients into something truly special.

◆

4 pork loin chops
Salt and freshly-milled black pepper
25g/1 oz butter
300ml/½ pt dry cider
1 dessert apple
½ teaspoon dried marjoram
150ml/¼ pt double cream

◆

Season the chops with salt and pepper. Melt the butter in a frying pan and quickly fry the chops so that they are golden brown on both sides. Pour over the cider, add the apple and marjoram, cover the pan and simmer gently for 20 minutes. Lift the chops out of the pan and arrange on a serving dish. Quickly boil up the liquor in the pan until it is reduced by about a quarter, then remove from the heat, stir in the cream and reheat. Taste and adjust the seasoning, pour over the chops and serve.

Serves 4

WILTSHIRE PORKIES

These little deep-fried sausagemeat balls in batter are wonderful served with a piquant sauce with drinks. As with so many other recipes, the use of high quality sausagemeat is of paramount importance.

◆

75g/3 oz plain flour
25g/1 oz self-raising flour
½ teaspoon salt
1 egg
150ml/¼ pt milk
675g/1½ lb sausagemeat
Seasoned flour
Fat or oil for deep frying

◆

Sift the flours and salt into a bowl. Make a well in the centre and drop in the egg together with about 3 tablespoons of the milk. Beat well, then gradually beat in the remaining milk.

Form the sausagemeat into balls about the size of an unshelled almond. Dip in the seasoned flour, then the batter and fry quickly in hot fat or oil until golden brown. Remove from the pan, drain on kitchen paper and serve as soon as possible.

Makes about 25

LOVE IN DISGUISE

A romantic West Country name, dating from the eighteenth century, which, in the past, has enticed people into eating a dish they might otherwise have rejected out of hand – namely stuffed heart. Of all offal, heart has the mildest flavour, but the idea of eating it puts some people off, so if it is served up sliced in a thick tomato sauce they are likely to have eaten at least their first mouthful before actually discovering what it is. Do make sure that you cook the hearts really well – overcooking is better than undercooking. Like many other casserole dishes, 'Love in Disguise' also improves in flavour if it is left overnight and is then reheated.

◆

4 small pigs' hearts
50g/2 oz butter
1 small onion, peeled and finely chopped
100g/4 oz fresh white breadcrumbs
4 tablespoons chopped parsley
Grated rind of 1 large lemon
1 egg, beaten
Salt and freshly-milled black pepper
1 tablespoon seasoned flour
400g/14 oz can tomatoes
4 tablespoons vegetable or chicken stock
1 tablespoon red wine vinegar
2 bay leaves
1 tablespoon mild English grain mustard
150ml/¼ pt double cream

◆

Wash the hearts under cold running water, then cut out any fat, gristle or arteries. Put to soak in lightly-salted water while preparing the stuffing.

Melt half the butter in a small pan and gently fry the onion for 5 minutes. Remove from the heat and stir in the breadcrumbs, parsley and lemon rind. Bind together with the egg and season well with salt and pepper. Remove the hearts from the brine, wipe dry and stuff with the breadcrumb mixture. Secure the openings with cocktail sticks then toss in the seasoned flour.

Purée the tomatoes in a blender or food processor, or sieve. Melt the remaining butter in a fireproof casserole and fry the hearts until very lightly browned. Pour over the tomatoes, stock and vinegar and bring to the boil. Add the bay leaves, cover tightly with foil and then the lid of the pan and cook in a very moderate oven, 150°C/300°F/Gas Mark 2 for 3 hours.

Lift the hearts out of the sauce, arrange them on individual serving plates and cut into thin slices. Stir the mustard and cream into the tomato sauce. Reheat gently without boiling then taste and adjust the seasoning. Pour the sauce over the hearts and serve at once.

Serves 4

CHAPTER FIVE
THE SOUTH AND SOUTH-EAST

The New Forest was one of the last remaining habitats of the wild boar in England and one of the last places where the pigs would spend the autumn being fattened on beech mast. The resultant Hampshire hams were highly prized because of their slightly nutty flavour.

The Black Berkshire pigs, one of the few remaining old breeds, originated in this part of England and, of those that still remain, the majority are still in the south east. Exactly how this breed came about seems open to question. Some say it was the result of crossing an Old English pig with a wild boar, others a Chinese pig with a wild boar and mention is even made of a cross with a pig from Barbados! This comparatively small pig with prick ears, however he came into being, was unquestionably a good 'doer' who enjoyed grazing and wandering about.

While there are no well known bacon or ham cures from this region, curing would have been carried out as elsewhere in England. William Cobbett particularly approved of the Hampshire method of burning off the hair, rather than scalding as was carried out in most other parts of the country. Scalding, he said, 'slackens the skin, opens all the pores of it, makes it loose and flabby by drawing out the roots of the hair'. Whereas singeing 'tightens the skin in every part, contracts all the sinews and veins in the skin, makes the flitch a solider thing'.

I found reading his *Cottage Economy* quite fascinating and above all enjoyed this passage: 'A couple of flitches of bacon are worth fifty thousand Methodist sermons and religious tracts. The sight of them upon the rack tends more to keep a man from poaching and stealing than whole volumes of penal statutes, though assisted by the terrors of the hulks and gibbet. They are the softeners of the temper, and promoters of domestic harmony.'

Social life for all but the aristocracy was very limited in the Middle Ages and Tudor Britain. Fairs were the highlight of the social calendar, whether they were local village fairs or bigger events lasting several days and to which people travelled miles. Over the years, certain foods became connected with different fairs. At the Maidhiring Fair held the week after Christmas at Launceston in Cornwall, ginger-flavoured biscuits, called Cornish fairings, were traditional. Cheese was the food served at the Wensleydale Fair and Roast Pork at St Bartholomew's Fair in London. This would seem to be appropriate as the fields where the fair was held later became Smithfield.

Smithfield was originally a live meat market to which animals were brought from all over the British Isles. The conditions under which the poor creatures must have had to travel and live when they arrived in London does not bear contemplation. As the population increased, Smithfield eventually became too small and the live market was moved to Copenhagen Fields (now the Caledonian Road). Smithfield became, as it is today, the premier meat market for dead carcasses in England. As a postscript, it should also be said that the coming of the railways enabled the animals to be slaughtered in the country and the carcasses then to be despatched by train to London.

London's cosmopolitan life has always attracted people from all over the world. No sooner do they arrive than they pick up our way of doing things, combine it with a time-honoured method from their own country and, before you can blink, they are doing things far better than we do! It will consequently come as no surprise that some of the best sausages in the home counties are being made by a Czech in south west London who won the Evening Standard Award for the best sausages in London not long ago. Emory St Marcus makes a wide range of sausages, as well as his own excellent pure pork ones and he uses interesting combinations of other meats as well as pork.

St Marcus, 1 Rockingham Close, London SW15 5RW
Tel: 01–878 1898 Open 8–6 seven days a week.

LONDON PARTICULAR

A thick pea and bacon soup, so called because it resembled the smogs of London, as Dickens aptly explained in *Bleak House*.

'I asked him whether there was a great fire anywhere? For the streets were so full of dense brown smoke that scarcely anything was to be seen.
"Oh dear no, miss" he said. "This is a London Particular."
I had never heard of such a thing.
"A fog, miss" said the young gentleman.
"O indeed!" said I.'

This recipe starts from scratch, using a bacon knuckle, but it is one of the best ways I know of utilizing bacon stock after boiling a joint. Also, if you have a few pieces of cooked bacon you can add at the end, so much the better.

◆

500g/1 lb 2 oz green or yellow split peas
1 knuckle of bacon or gammon
25g/1 oz butter
2 large onions, peeled and chopped
2 carrots, peeled and chopped
1.8 l./3 pt water
1 bouquet garni
Salt and freshly-milled black pepper

◆

Put the peas into a bowl, cover them with cold water and leave to soak overnight, then drain well. Unless the knuckle is very salty, it is unnecessary to soak it overnight. Put into a pan, cover with cold water and bring to the boil. Remove from the heat and drain. Melt the butter in a large pan, add the onion and carrots and cook gently for 5 minutes. Pour in the water and bring to the boil, then add the peas, bacon and bouquet garni. Cover the pan and simmer gently for about 2½ hours or until the peas are very mushy. Lift out the bacon knuckle and bouquet garni. Remove the skin of the bacon and finely chop the meat, discarding the bone. Add to the soup and reheat gently. Taste and adjust the seasoning, adding a little salt if necessary and plenty of freshly-milled black pepper.

Serves 6–8

KENTISH GAMMON WITH CHERRIES

A typical recipe from 'The Garden of England' incorporating fruit with gammon steak. As this is the kind of recipe which makes a marvellous, quickly-prepared meal for two, quantities are given for just two steaks, but they can obviously be increased if wished.

◆

2 gammon steaks
Freshly-milled black pepper
25g/1 oz butter
100g/4 oz ripe cherries, stoned
2 tablespoons port

◆

Season the gammon steaks with pepper. Melt the butter in a large frying pan and quickly fry the steaks until golden brown on both sides. Lower the heat, add the cherries together with the port, cover the pan and simmer gently together for 5 minutes before serving.

Serves 2

SKUETS

The British are brilliant at adopting the cuisines of other nations. So much so that the majority of people today think the practice of threading meat on to skewers and cooking over an open fire originated in Greece and Turkey where they are called kebabs, kabobs and other similar names. The truth is that this was how man cooked his food from the beginning of time all over the world, first by using twigs (as in Indonesian sate) and then in the Bronze and Iron Ages progressing to primitive skewers.

Through simple necessity, it was developed into an art form during the reign of Richard II. One of his 300 cooks had a silversmith produce some beautifully crafted, elegant little skewers on which a variety of little titbits were threaded.

Coriander had been introduced to Britain by the Romans but by the time of Richard II, the spice route from the East, bringing ginger, nutmeg, mace etc., was well established. It was a long slow journey which inevitably meant high prices for the spices at the end of it. They were seized upon with great delight on their arrival in London for not only did they improve the flavour of fresh meat, they also disguised meat that was tainted! With less flavour in much of our meat today, we are inevitably having to resort to an increased use of herbs and spices. Their judicious use can transform a really simple dish such as this.

450g/1 lb lean pork
2 pig's kidneys
Salt and freshly-milled black pepper
1 teaspoon ground coriander
½ teaspoon ground ginger
½ teaspoon ground mace
25g/1 oz butter, melted

Cut the pork into 1.25-cm/½-in dice. Cut the kidneys in half, remove the cores and cut into the same size pieces as the pork. Put into a bowl, scatter over the salt and pepper, add the spices and mix well together. Thread the meat on to four skewers, then leave in a cool place for about 6 hours to allow the flavours to really penetrate. Brush all over with the melted butter and grill for about 15 minutes, turning several times. Serve hot.

Serves 4

BACON FROISE

Spelt in a variety of different ways, including fraze, fraise and frayses, this is a dish which was popular from medieval times through until the eighteenth century. A cross between an omelette and a pancake, its closest relation is possibly the Spanish tortilla. While bacon froise is the most common, other fillings such as chicken were sometimes used as well.

◆

2 eggs
25g/1 oz flour
150ml/¼ pt single cream
Salt and freshly-milled black pepper
25g/1 oz butter
6 rashers streaky bacon, de-rinded and chopped
1 medium-sized onion, peeled and chopped

◆

Beat the eggs, then whisk in the flour. When the mixture is smooth, gradually beat in the cream. Season with a little salt and plenty of pepper and put on one side. Melt half the butter in a small pan and gently fry the bacon and onion for 10 minutes.

Heat the remaining butter in a 17.5-cm/7-in frying pan. Pour in the egg mixture and cook over a moderate heat for 5 minutes, then scatter over the bacon and onion mixture. Cook for a further 2–3 minutes. Gently slide the froise out of the pan on to a plate. Invert the frying pan on to the plate and tip it up so that the uncooked side of the froise is on the base of the pan. Replace over the heat and cook for 5 minutes until the under side is golden brown. Remove from the heat and serve as soon as possible.

Serves 2–3

CHAPTER SIX
THE MIDLANDS
◆

Stretching in a wide band from Herefordshire in the west across to Leicestershire in the east, this part of England has always been renowned for its pork dishes. The Midlands have also produced two of the best known breeds of pig, the Gloucester Old Spot and the Tamworth.

Known as the orchard pig, the Gloucester Old Spot favoured life among the apple orchards of the Evesham Vale and the cider-growing county of Hereford. It used to be said that the dappled spots of his skin were a natural camouflage as he rooted amongst the sunlit orchards with patches of light and shade. This is purely folklore. The earlier Gloucester pig had very few markings on it and the spots appeared through cross-breeding with a black pig! What is true is that he is a pig who thrives on windfall apples to fatten him from the late summer through until the harvest. A diet which would not suit other pigs.

From the north and east Midlands came the Tamworth pig, considered by many to be the finest among the old breeds. Numbers did fall dangerously low, with only seventeen boars being registered by the Rare Breeds Survival Trust in 1976. However, stocks are now on the increase and they are being used extensively by farmers wishing to return to older methods of meat production.

Both these pigs, as well as Iron Age Pigs and other very rare breeds, can be seen at the Cotswold Farm Park at Guiting Power in Gloucestershire. Marvellous work has been done here in saving not only pigs, but other breeds of farm animal from extinction and many of their progeny have been sent to other parts of the British Isles and throughout the world. The place is a sheer delight for children as the animals are all tame. You can walk right up to the fences to see them whilst others, like the piglets, are allowed to run about freely.

The Midlands do not have any well-known bacon or ham cures, although many years ago there was a Gloucester ham, a Tewksbury ham and an Oxfordshire ham which was cured in beer. However, there are some butchers who still do their own dry-salted bacon and hams, such as Ralph's in Melton Mowbray, whose black pudding we much enjoyed. There is a wide variety of regional sausages including the Gloucestershire, Oxford and the Leicestershire Tomato Sausage (page 29), as well as Lincolnshire sausages near the county boundary.

In the Black Country, faggots are very popular and I was assured by Keith Boxley of Wombourne (page 44) that Faggots with Mushy Peas are an essential ingredient of a 'Black Country Man's Night Out', when served in paper cups and eaten with a spoon while watching a show in a pub. He also explained that the same combination used to be taken to work in a tin, wrapped up in a cloth to conserve the heat, as the mid-day meal for the mill workers.

One has to travel to the eastern part of the region though to find its most famed product, the Melton Mowbray Pork Pie (page 34). A good, home-made pork pie bears as much resemblance to the limp, plastic-wrapped object one buys in the supermarket as a designer dress does to the cheap copy bought in the high street chain.

Simple food it may be, but a really good pork pie takes a lot of beating. The problem is that they were not designed for these days of refrigeration, freezing and transportation from one end of the country to another. To experience them at their best, they should be baked and eaten within a couple of days.

The Cotswold Farm Park (over) Guiting Power,
Cheltenham, Gloucestershire. Tel: (04515) 307
Open 10.30–6.00 Easter to end September.

Dickinson & Morris 10 Nottingham Street,
Melton Mowbray, Leicestershire. Tel: (0664) 62341
Open 8.30–5 Monday to Saturday.

Ralph's Butchers (page 80) 16 Market Place, Melton
Mowbray, Leicestershire. Tel: (0664) 62955
Open 8.30–5 Monday to Saturday.

Keith Boxley (over) Wombourn, Staffordshire. Tel: (0902) 892359.

GAMMON WITH APRICOTS

Whole hams, baked and stuffed with apricots, were traditionally served at the annual wool fairs in Oxfordshire. It was here that the famous Moor Park strain of apricot was developed. It is likely that the idea of serving ham with apricots and peaches, so popular today in the United States, was taken out from England by the early settlers.

At this time of the year, the apricots would have been slightly under-ripe, so they were lightly cooked until the juice ran out before stuffing. If fresh apricots are unavailable, use 175-g/6-oz dried apricots soaked overnight in water. Half hams are very difficult to obtain other than at Christmas, so I have suggested using a 1.8-kg/4-lb piece of gammon. I tried cooking this in the traditional Oxfordshire way in a huff paste but as gammon is always brine-cured, even if it has no other added water, too much liquid escapes for it to be successful. I think a better result is achieved by wrapping it in foil.

◆

1.8kg/4 lb piece of gammon
225g/8 oz apricots (see above)
2 tablespoons water (see above)
100g/4 oz fresh white breadcrumbs
Freshly-milled black pepper
8 cloves
3 tablespoons honey

◆

Cut out the bone from the gammon and place the gammon in a large bowl. Cover with cold water and leave to soak for 4 hours. Remove the stones from the apricots and chop the apricots roughly. Put into a pan with the water and cook for about 4 minutes, or until the juice starts to run. If using previously-soaked dried apricots, dry them, then chop into several pieces. Mix the apricots with the breadcrumbs and season lightly with pepper. Press the apricot stuffing into the cavity where the bone was removed.

Lay out a sheet of foil on a work surface large enough to completely envelop the gammon. Scatter half the cloves over the foil. Spread the honey evenly all over the gammon and lay the gammon in the centre. Sprinkle over the remaining cloves. Bring up the edges of the foil to completely enclose it. Put into a baking tin and bake in a moderate oven, 180°C/350°F/Gas Mark 4 for 2 hours. Remove from the oven and allow to cool.

When the gammon is completely cold, unwrap and peel off the rind.

Serves 8–12

FEBRUARY PORK PUDDING

What is perhaps slightly surprising about this Northamptonshire recipe is that it uses fresh pork rather than bacon or salt pork; a more likely choice for a post-Christmas dish.

◆

675g/1½ lb lean shoulder of pork
2 large leeks
1 medium-sized potato
1 teaspoon dried sage
Salt and freshly-milled black pepper
350g/12 oz suet crust pastry (page 141)
150ml/¼ pt light ale

◆

Cut the pork into 2-cm/¾-in pieces and put them into a bowl. Trim the leeks, wash thoroughly, cut in half lengthways then chop. Peel the potato, cut into 0.25-cm/¼-in dice and add to the pork in the bowl. Sprinkle over the sage and season well with salt and pepper.

Roll out three-quarters of the pastry and use to line a greased 1.8-l./3-pt pudding basin. Fill with the pork and leek mixture, then pour over the ale. Roll out the remaining pastry to a circle for a lid.

Dampen the pastry edges with water, lift on the lid and seal and trim the edges. Cover first with a layer of greased greaseproof paper and then a layer of foil, making a pleat in the top to allow the pudding to expand. Steam for 4 hours, checking from time to time to make sure that the pan does not boil dry. Serve with a little gravy.

Serves 4–6

STUFFED LEG OF PORK WITH HARICOT BEANS

A slightly unusual way of cooking traditional roast pork with sage and onion stuffing, which was given to me by Mrs Chainey of Bromyard, Herefordshire. To ensure that the lean of the meat stays really moist, the joint is first boiled for an hour before boning, stuffing and roasting. Haricot beans are then added to the pork stock to cook while the joint is roasting and, according to Mrs Chainey, in true Hereford style the pork and beans should then be accompanied by 'home-grown vegetables and home-brewed cider'.

◆

Half a leg of pork weighing about 2.25kg/5 lb
2 teaspoons salt
1 bouquet garni
boiling water
450g/1 lb onions
4 oz fresh white breadcrumbs
1 tablespoon fresh sage or 1 teaspoon dried
Freshly-milled black pepper
225–350g/8–12 oz haricot beans, previously soaked overnight in cold water
15g/½ oz lard or 1 tablespoon oil

◆

Place the joint in a large pan with the salt and bouquet garni. Pour over enough boiling water to just cover the joint, then cover with a lid and simmer very gently for 1 hour.

Peel the onions, add them to the pan and simmer them for 15–20 minutes, depending on their size. Lift out of the pan with a draining spoon and, when cool enough to handle, chop the onions finely. Put into a basin with the breadcrumbs and sage, mix well together and season to taste.

Carefully lift the pork out of the pan on to a board and leave for about 15 minutes, or until cool enough to handle. With a small sharp knife, cut out the bone of the pork and put this back into the pork stock. Add the haricot beans to the pan, bring to the boil and boil rapidly for 10 minutes, then reduce the heat and simmer gently for 1½ hours.

Stuff the cavity where the bone was removed and place the joint on a rack in a roasting tin. Lightly dot the lean with lard or brush with a little oil and season with salt and pepper. Place in a moderately hot oven, 190°C/375°F/Gas Mark 5 for 1½ hours, basting the joint from time to time.

Remove from the oven and allow to stand for 5 minutes before carving, while the gravy is made from the pan juices together with some of the stock from the beans. Drain the beans and serve with the pork.

Serves 8 (or more if there are children.)

QUORN BACON ROLL

For the mounted hunt followers in Leicestershire, the day would start with a hunt breakfast. During the day they would be sustained with wedges of Melton Mowbray pork pie and at the end of the day's exertions they would retire home to a substantial tea. Less fortunate were the hunt servants, grooms and kennelmen. They would have to prepare the horses, travel to the meet, ride a second horse for their masters all day, and, on their return, would still have to see their charges safely back in their stables and kennels before they could stop and eat.

After such a long day, a hot filling meal was essential and this bacon roll was traditional fare. This particular version must be post 1883 as golden syrup was not invented until then. It may sound unusual but do not be tempted to omit it as it makes the roll into something just a little more special.

◆

350g/12 oz suet pastry (page 141)
450g/1 lb streaky bacon
2 onions, peeled and finely chopped
1 teaspoon fresh thyme or ¼ teaspoon dried thyme
1 teaspoon chopped fresh sage or ¼ teaspoon dried sage
Freshly-milled black pepper
1 generous tablespoon golden syrup

◆

Roll the suet pastry out to a rectangle about 25x17.5cm/10x7 in.

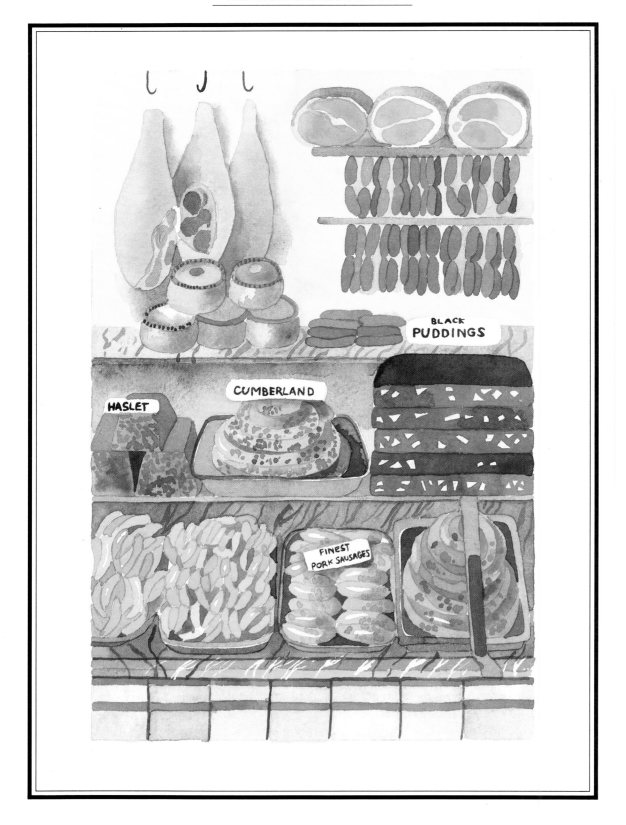

De-rind the bacon and cut each rasher into about 6 pieces. Scatter evenly over the pastry to within 2.4cm/1 in of the edge all the way round. Cover with the onion, herbs and pepper. Finally, pour the golden syrup down the centre in a long line.

Roll up the pastry, like a Swiss roll. Wrap first in a piece of greased greaseproof paper, then a double thickness of foil. Place in a large pan or steamer and steam for 3 hours.

Remove from the steamer, take off the covers and place on a serving plate. Then put into a low oven for 5 minutes, just to allow the pastry to dry out a little. Serve hot.

Serves 6–8

COTSWOLD PORK WITH ORANGE

Pot roasting always produces a beautifully tender, well-flavoured meat and this dish is no exception. It does not, however, produce good crackling, so if the joint has crackling, this should be removed with a sharp knife. It can then be salted and cooked at a later time in a moderately hot oven, 200°C/400°F/Gas Mark 6 for about 1 hour or until crisp. Remove from the oven, break into small pieces and sprinkle with herbs, spices or seasonings of your choice and serve with drinks.

◆

25g/1 oz butter
1 large cooking apple, peeled and sliced
2 medium-sized onions, peeled and sliced
900g/2 lb joint shoulder pork, boned and rolled
25g/1 oz seasoned flour
1 orange
2 teaspoons chopped fresh oregano or ½ teaspoon dried oregano
300ml/½ pt boiling stock or water
Salt and freshly-milled black pepper

◆

Melt the butter in a large frying pan and gently fry the onion and apple for 5 minutes. Lift out of the pan with a draining spoon and place in a casserole with a lid.

Coat the joint with the seasoned flour. Increase the heat in the frying pan and fry the meat until it is golden brown all over. Lift out of the pan and place in the casserole. Very thinly peel the rind off the orange and cut into fine matchstick strips. Scatter over the pork. Using a sharp knife, peel the orange, removing all the skin and pith and divide into segments. Do this over a basin to catch all the juice and squeeze out all the juice from the pith remaining. Add to the apple and onion with the oregano.

Pour over the boiling stock or water, cover the casserole first with a piece of foil and then the lid and cook in a low oven, 150°C/300°F/Gas Mark 2 for 3 hours. Lift out the pork, cut into slices and arrange on a serving plate. Taste and adjust the seasoning of the stock then spoon over the pork with the onion, apple and orange.

Serves 4

THE SHERIFF'S STEAK

This recipe was given to me by Ralph's Butchers in Melton Mowbray. They sell an excellent range of sausages and home-cured, dry-salted bacon as well as these little packages ready for cooking at home.

◆

4 pork escalopes, weighing about 100g/4 oz each
100g/4 oz Stilton cheese
2 tablespoons single cream
1 dessert apple, peeled and chopped
1 egg, beaten
2 tablespoons seasoned flour
75g/3 oz fresh white or brown breadcrumbs
Butter and oil for frying

◆

If the pork has not already been flattened, place it between two sheets of damp greaseproof paper. Hit with a meat mallet or rolling pin until it is as thin as possible but try not to tear it. Mash the cheese in a basin with the cream and stir in the apple. Divide into four. Spread the cheese mixture over one half of each escalope to within 0.75cm/¼ in of the edge. Brush the edge of the meat with a little of the egg and fold over the unstuffed half so that the filling is completely enclosed and resembles a parcel.

Dip each parcel first in seasoned flour, then the remaining egg and finally in the breadcrumbs so that it is evenly coated. Shallow fry in a mixture of butter and oil for about 10 minutes, turning once. The crumb should be golden brown. If it is becoming too dark, reduce the heat, as it is important to ensure that the meat is thoroughly cooked. Lift out of the pan with a fish slice and serve hot.

Serves 4

BLACK PUDDING ON TOAST

Continental cookery books, especially French, abound with recipes for using black pudding in simple country soups and casseroles, or in recipes such as the celebrated Normandy dish of Black Pudding, Calvados and Apples. In England, it is generally just served fried. However, this recipe from Shropshire makes a good quick snack which will be enjoyed by people who love black pudding and may convert one or two who are a bit dubious! Remember, start with a good black pudding in the first place, not one which is full of rusk.

◆

175g/6 oz black pudding
25g/1 oz butter
1 medium-sized onion, peeled and finely chopped
1 rounded tablespoon medium oatmeal
1 tablespoon chopped parsley
Salt and freshly-milled black pepper
2 buttered rounds of toast

◆

Take the skin off the black pudding and mash the pudding. Melt the butter in a pan and gently fry the onion for 5 minutes. Stir in the oatmeal and continue cooking for a couple of minutes, then add the black pudding. Blend in well and cook for a further 2-3 minutes, stirring. Add the parsley and season to taste with salt and pepper. Pile on to the two pieces of toast and serve at once.

Serves 2

COUNTY SAUCE

A spicy tomato sauce from Leicestershire which was traditionally served with the local pork pies.

◆

450g/1 lb tomatoes
450g/1 lb cooking apples
450g/1 lb onions
Peeled rind and juice 1 lemon
175g/6 oz sultanas
175g/6 oz sugar
2 tablespoons salt
2 tablespoons mixed spice
900ml/1½ pt distilled malt vinegar

◆

Roughly chop the tomatoes, apples and onions and put into a pan with all the remaining ingredients. Place over a gentle heat until the sugar has dissolved, stirring frequently, then cover and simmer gently for 45 minutes. Purée in a blender or food processor and then rub through a non-metal sieve. Tip the sauce back into the pan and boil rapidly until it is reduced by about a quarter. Pour into sterilized jars or bottles and seal

Makes about 1.2 l./2 pt

CHAPTER SEVEN
EAST ANGLIA
◆

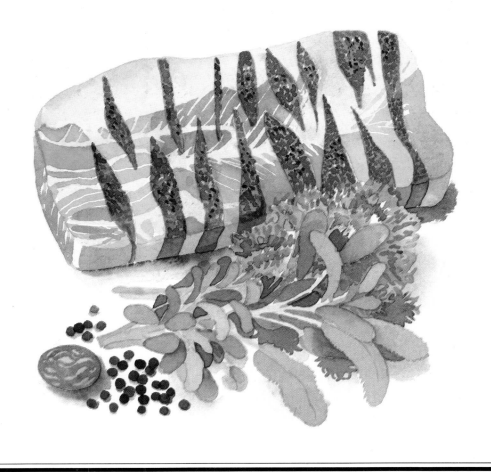

The pig is not over-fond of water, so he would not have enjoyed life on the fens of East Anglia before the dykes drained them. All other aspects of this flat part of England suited him well. The arable land ensured a plentiful supply of food. Following the harvest, pigs would have been able to forage on the stubble to fatten themselves and then they could be kept through the winter on root vegetables which are grown extensively. Pig farming grew and with it, the pork butchers. Almost every town still boasts at least one specialist pork butcher. In Newmarket, where I now live, we have two as well as a delicatessen selling Musk's sausages (see page 86).

The Essex, the indigenous pig, is now extinct, but he was a direct descendant of the Anglo-Saxon and Norman pigs which foraged in the forests. Epping and Thetford are about the only two still remaining and they are considerably diminished in size. Large Blacks also originated in East Anglia, though possibly with some West Country influence as well. Whilst the numbers of them are few, there are still people rearing the odd one or two, as well as a few farms with pedigree herds.

Suffolk is famed for its sweetcure bacon and hams. A number of butchers still cure their own bacon and amongst the best of these is Edis of Ely, though actually in Bury St Edmunds! (His brother who has the shop in Ely makes superb pork pies.) The dark treacle coating of the sweetcure gives the bacon an unusually dark appearance but it has marvellous flavour and, while waiting in the queue, you can nibble at their delicious pork scratchings. Crisp and salty, they make an excellent snack to serve with drinks and do not remotely resemble the synthesized ones bought in packets.

Emmett's Store is one of the most remarkable little shops I have ever visited. Set in the picturesque village of Peasenhall in the heart of rural Suffolk, it remains a typical village store, selling everything from groceries to stationery, underwear, clothes and knitting wools! They also supply Queen Elizabeth the Queen Mother with hams and proudly display the Royal Warrant. The hams and bacon really are quite superb and, over the years, they have built up a large mail-order clientele, apart from the locals who pop in for a pound of bacon.

The exact recipe is a family secret. Basically, the hams are first put into a wet brine for a week, then into pickling casks for three to four weeks when they are turned every day. They have two different pickles, one made with stout and treacle together with herbs and spices and the other with apple juice and cider from the local cider mill. After pickling, they are hung to dry for a couple of days and finally smoked over oak sawdust for a week.

If you want to buy a whole ham from them, which I would thoroughly recommend, I would advise buying one with a bit of fat on as these hams really do benefit from it. They sell them cooked or uncooked, but if buying uncooked, give them plenty of soaking before cooking. They recommend overnight but I think they need twenty-four hours if they are to be boiled or thirty-six if you cook them in foil or a huff crust as I did.

After smoking, the Peasenhall hams are not left to mature (although they can be, and often are, kept for several months) unlike the Suffolk Seager ham which requires five–seven months. Created by Mr Robert Seager of Ipswich over a hundred years ago, the recipe for making them was bought by the Harris Bacon Company.

They continued making them in the traditional manner, using small hams and a similar method to the Jerreys until the 1970s when they ceased production. Having successfully started making Bradenham hams again at their factory in Leeming Bar in 1987, they also re-introduced the Seager, which has proved extremely popular.

At one time there was also a Norfolk ham which was smoked over seaweed giving it a very distinctive flavour. This has not been seen for some time but it is not impossible that some enterprising person may seize on the idea and start producing it again.

A visit to a pork butcher's shop in Lincolnshire, such as Nelson's in Stamford, is a real delight. Here they take their pork products seriously and there is an array of sausages, pies, Bath chaps, jellied pork, brawn – in fact just about anything that can be made from a pig is made! Game is also plentiful in this part of England and many recipes combine both pork or bacon with the game. A classic French as well as English combination.

Emmett's Store (over) Peasenhall, Suffolk IP17 2HJ
Tel: (072879) 250. Open 8.30–5.30 (closed 1–1.30)
Monday to Friday, 5 p.m. Saturday. Also mail order.

Harris – Leeming Bar (above) Leeming Bar,
Northallerton, Yorkshire DL7 9AW Tel: (0677) 22661
Telephone orders or mail order.

Edis of Ely (page 84) 4 St John's Street, Bury St
Edmunds, Suffolk IP33 1SQ Tel: (0284) 3297
Open 8–5 Tuesday, Wednesday, Friday, to 1 Thursday,
7–5 Saturday.

Edis of Ely (page 84) 24 High Street
Ely CB7 4JU Tel: (0353) 2757
Open 9–5 Monday, Wednesday, to 1 Tuesday,
8.30–5.30 Thursday, Friday, 8–5 Saturday.

Nelson's Butchers (page 85) 8 Red Lion
Square, Stamford, Lincolnshire PE9 2AJ Tel: (0780) 62344
and 37 Broad Street, Stamford, Lincolnshire PE9 1PL
Tel: (0780) 63414. Also branches at Oakham and Uppingham
in Leicestershire. Open 7–5 Monday to Saturday.

A S Curtis & Sons (page 88) 164 High Street, Lincoln
LN5 7AF Tel: (0522) 30802 Open 8.30–5.30 Monday to Saturday.

Musk's of Newmarket (page 84) 1 The Rookery,
Newmarket, Suffolk CB8 8EQ Tel: (0638) 661824
Open 9–5 Monday to Saturday. Closed 1–2 and
Wednesday afternoon.

Parkinson's 6 West Street, Crowland,
Cambridgeshire PE6 OED Tel: (0733) 210233
Open 8–5.30 Tuesday to Saturday. Closed Monday.

SUFFOLK SMOKED SAUSAGE AND RED CABBAGE CASSEROLE

Having found a number of recipes from Suffolk using sausages and red cabbage, I decided to try one using some of the delicious smoked sausages I had bought from Emmett's Stores in Peasenhall (page 85). The nearest equivalent which is generally available are Polish cabanos and, although they will not give you such a strongly-flavoured dish, the result should still be excellent.

◆

25g/1 oz butter
1 medium-sized onion, peeled and chopped
100g/4 oz good quality smoked bacon, or sweetcure bacon,
de-rinded and chopped
2 sticks celery, chopped
900g/2 lb red cabbage, shredded
4 tablespoons vinegar
2 tablespoons soft brown sugar
150ml/¼ pt stock
350g/12 oz Suffolk smoked sausages or 450g/1 lb cabanos
(see above)
Salt and freshly-milled black pepper

◆

Melt the butter in a fireproof casserole and gently fry the onion, bacon and celery for 5 minutes. Increase the heat slightly, add the cabbage and toss for 1–2 minutes. Then add the vinegar, sugar and stock and bring to the boil.

Cover and place in a very moderate oven, 160°C/325°F/Gas Mark 3 for 1 hour. Add the sausages, keeping them whole if small or cutting into 10-cm/4-in lengths. Replace in the oven and cook for a further hour. Taste and adjust the seasoning before serving. It is important not to add the salt until this stage as the bacon and sausages can already be quite salty. Serve with jacket potatoes which can be placed in the oven at the same time as the casserole.

Serves 4

LINCOLNSHIRE CHINE

Chine really is one of few regional dishes left which is widely available within the county, but is barely known outside. Various reasons have been given for this but I can't help but feel that perhaps it has something to do with the smell. When made with fresh parsley, the lightly-cured meat with its lines of parsley stuffing is a real delicacy. However it has to be said that it smells awful.

Despite the fact that much of the production of chine is shrouded in mystery, with the help of the butcher at Curtis of Lincoln's main branch I was able to produce a very good one myself at home. Most Lincolnshire butchers cure the whole chine, i.e. instead of the pig being split down the middle, the head and shoulders are removed and then the whole chine or forerib is butchered out in one piece together with the backbone. This produces a piece of meat weighing about 6.75kg/14 lb. As this is rather larger than most people would want, I opted for buying half a chine, cut in the more usual way. This weighed only 2kg/4½ lb which is a more manageable size.

For those who have tried chine and enjoyed every mouthful but do not want to go to the bother of making it themselves, or for those curious enough to want to try it, it is not necessary to visit Lincolnshire. Curtis's will supply vacuum-packed cooked slices by mail order from their factory in Long Leys Road, Lincoln. They also sell the whole cured joints, ready for stuffing and cooking at home. They will send this on mail order by special request or, if you are in the vicinity, you can ring and order one and they will send it out to any one of their shops ready for collection. If you decide to do this, do not go home without at least one of their wonderful Lincolnshire Plum Breads!

◆

Half a chine or forerib, weighing about 2kg/4½ lb
3.6 l./6 pt all-purpose brine (page 49)
100g/4 oz fresh parsley
1 tablespoon chopped fresh sage
¼ teaspoon grated nutmeg
Freshly-milled black pepper

◆

Take the piece of meat and prick it all over with a carving fork. This helps the brine to soak into the meat, giving a more even cure. Put the meat into a suitable container. Pour over the brine and leave for 2–4 days.

Remove, allow to drain, put into a piece of muslin and leave to mature in the refrigerator for 3–4 days. Take out and make slits in the meat, down to the bone, about 2.5-cm/1-in apart. Wash the parsley very thoroughly to remove all the grit, put into a clean tea towel and wring dry, then chop. You can do this in a blender or food processor if you wish, but do not allow it to become too much of a mush. Add the sage and mix lightly, then the nutmeg and plenty of freshly-milled black pepper. Use this mixture to stuff the chine, making sure you press it right down next to the bone.

Wrap the chine in a piece of muslin and tie the ends. Place in a large pan, cover with cold water and bring to the boil. Simmer gently for 1¾ hours then remove from the heat and allow to cool for 3–4 hours in the cooking liquor. Remove and allow to drain, then press with a weighted board overnight.

To serve the chine, cut in thin slices across the meat towards the backbone. Do not worry if the slices break up slightly as they can then be reassembled on the serving plate.

Serves 8–10

DUNMOW BOILED BACON WITH BROAD BEANS

Great Dunmow in Essex is renowned for its presentation of the Dunmow Flitch, a custom dating back to the thirteenth century. In their desire to witness happy marriages amongst their flock, the monks at Dunmow Monastery guaranteed to provide any couple with a flitch, or side of bacon, if they could honestly prove that during the preceding 366 days they had never once had a cross word or for one second wished themselves unwed. History does not seem to relate how many flitches a year the monks had to part with, but presumably it was not too great a number or the tradition would not have survived so long. It was also perhaps a gentle reminder to them all that the life of celibacy they had chosen had many compensations!

◆

1.25kg/3 lb lean forehock or shoulder bacon joint
1 onion, peeled and quartered
1 small carrot, peeled and roughly chopped
1 bay leaf
Salt
450g/1 lb shelled broad beans
40g/1½ oz flour
200ml/8 fl oz milk
3 tablespoons chopped parsley
Freshly-milled black pepper

◆

Put the bacon joint into a pan of water, bring *slowly* to the boil then discard the water. Cover again with fresh cold water, add the onion, carrot and bay leaf and bring slowly back to the boil. Cover the pan and simmer gently for 1½ hours. Remove the bacon from the pan, put on to a heated serving dish and keep warm.

Strain some of the bacon stock into a clean pan and add salt, if necessary. Bring to the boil, add the beans and cook for about 8 minutes or until just tender. Drain thoroughly, reserving the water.

Melt the butter in a pan, stir in the flour and cook for a minute, then gradually stir in the milk and 200ml/8 fl oz of the bean stock. Bring to the boil, stirring all the time, then stir in the parsley and beans. Season to taste with black pepper and serve the beans with the boiled bacon.

Serves 6

LINCOLNSHIRE HARSLET

When I told a photographer and art director, who both come from Lincolnshire, that I was writing this book, they both proceeded to wax lyrically about Chine (page 88) and Harslet. The spelling being all important, as in other parts of the country it is spelt and pronounced haslet.

Although it is made elsewhere, it is in East Anglia that its popularity has remained undiminished with the march of time and progress. Indeed, Scott's in York make a delicious one with fresh and pickled pork added to it which, as well as adding flavour, gives it an attractive pink tinge.

Similar to faggots (page 44) but without the breadcrumbs, the other differences are that it is baked as a loaf, rather than being separated into small balls and it is more usually served cold, cut in slices.

◆

450g/1 lb pig's pluck (page 42)
450g/1 lb lean pork
225g/8 oz pork fat
675g/1½ lb onions
2 tablespoons chopped fresh sage or 2 teaspoons dried sage
Salt and freshly-milled black pepper
1 pig's caul
50g/2 oz lard

◆

Either mince the pluck, lean pork, pork fat and onions or put into a blender or food processor. If using a food processor, cut the fat into very small pieces and put into the processor with the lean pork so that it does not clog up. Add the sage and seasoning. Soak the caul in tepid water for about 15 minutes then lay it out on a working surface. Form the minced mixture into a loaf, lay on top of the caul and wrap it round so the minced mixture is completely enclosed.

Place in a roasting tin and dot with the lard. Roast in a moderately hot oven, 200°C/400°F/Gas Mark 6 for 1 hour or until browned. Allow to cool. Serve cold, cut in slices.

Serves 10–12

HUNTINGDON FIDGET PIE

The word fidget derives from flitch, i.e. a side of bacon. A variety of fidget pies are made throughout England. Besides the Huntingdon one, the best known is the Shropshire pie which also contains potato.

◆

450g/1 lb streaky bacon, de-rinded and chopped
225g/8 oz onions, peeled and chopped
450g/1 lb Bramley cooking apples, peeled, cored and chopped
Freshly-milled black pepper and salt if necessary
150ml/¼ pt cider
225g/8 oz short crust pastry (page 140)
Beaten egg for glazing

◆

Mix the bacon, onion and apple together and turn into a 1.2-l./2-pt pie dish. Season with freshly-milled black pepper and a little salt, depending on the saltiness of the bacon, and pour over the cider.

Roll out the pastry and use to cover the pie. Brush all over with beaten egg to glaze and bake in a hot oven, 200°C/400°F/Gas Mark 6 for 20 minutes. Then lower the temperature to 180°C/350°F/Gas Mark 4 for a further 30 minutes. Serve hot.

Serves 4

GAME (PIE)

In Edwardian times a pie did not have to have a crust. All that was necessary in order for it to be deemed a pie was for it to be baked in the oven in a dish like a pie dish. You can use any game you like, including pheasant, partridge, wild duck or hare. All that you have to make sure is that you have approximately 225g/8 oz meat for mincing with the pork, and 225g/8 oz of breast fillets or slices of hare from the saddle, for the centre.

◆

225g/8 oz game meat from the breast or saddle of hare (see above)
Salt and freshly-milled black pepper
2 tablespoons brandy
175g/6 oz game meat from the legs and back
175g/6 oz pork shoulder or spare rib (it just wants a little fat to it)
175g/6 oz salt pork belly
3 shallots, very finely chopped
1½ teaspoons fresh thyme
2 tablespoons chopped parsley
4 tablespoons red wine
50g/2 oz breadcrumbs
4 rashers smoked streaky bacon, de-rinded

◆

Cut the breast fillets or saddle of hare into strips 1.25cm/½ in wide. Put into a bowl, season with salt and pepper then pour over the brandy and leave to marinate.

Either mince together the game meat, pork shoulder and pork belly or process in a blender or food processor. Turn into a bowl and mix well. Finely chop the shallots and add to the mixture with the thyme, parsley, red wine, breadcrumbs and seasoning. Mix thoroughly. Pack half the mixture into a lightly-greased terrine or pie dish. Lay the strips of meat on top, then the bacon rashers. Cover with the last of the minced mixture, pressing it down well. Cover securely, stand in a roasting tin containing 2.5cm/1 in of hot water and bake in a moderately hot oven, 180°C/350°F/Gas Mark 4 for 2 hours. Remove from the oven, stand a weight on top to press the mixture and leave overnight.

Serves 8

CHAPTER EIGHT
THE NORTH
◆

Robust is the term generally applied to northern food, but it is far from being all stodge as the recipes in this chapter prove. True, many recipes were cheap, nourishing dishes suitable for men and women who spent their lives doing hard manual labour, often under appalling conditions. These days, with a different lifestyle and a much wider choice of food available to us, we would possibly not want to eat them too often. But if well cooked they are still fun to have occasionally, especially on a cold winter's day. The north can also boast a number of elegant dishes such as Georgian marbled meats, left over from the days when Harrogate was almost as popular a spa town as Bath.

The most common breed of pig today is the Large White, which originated in Yorkshire. There were also Middle Whites which still exist in small numbers, and Small Whites which are now extinct. The Large White, a robust, hearty pig, was ideally suited to life in the Lake District and the Yorkshire Dales. He was also, apparently, quite a good walker. As Dorothy Hartley in *Food in England* says: 'We believe, from length of bone, that this pig was capable of walking long distances from hill farms to market without undue fatigue or loss of weight.'

One would presume though that these were not the over-fattened pigs, beloved of so many northerners. Joanna Bradshaw of Pockling, Yorkshire, told me that while pigs were generally killed at 254kg/560 lb her parents can remember one being killed at the village of Fryton which weighed 558kg/1,232 lb and that people travelled from all the surrounding villages just to see it!

Whatever may be said about the north's black puddings (and if you want a good black puddding this is where you have to come), the York ham must rate as the finest pork product of this region. It is famed not only throughout the British Isles but all over the world. Even the French call their unsmoked hams *Jambon d'York* after it.

What surprised me when I went to Yorkshire to find some genuine York hams is that they are not generally smoked. Every book I have ever read in which there is any mention of York hams says that the reason for their success was that during the 100 years it took to build York Minster, there was always a plentiful supply of oak sawdust to smoke the hams.

I mentioned this to Mr Bailey who now owns and runs Scott's in York, one of the few remaining butchers who still cure their own hams, and he laughed. As far as he and all the staff who worked there were aware (and some of them were not exactly spring chickens), the York ham was always an unsmoked or green ham. Clearly one cannot believe everything one reads!

Certainly the Marsh York ham, which is the one most widely available outside of the county, is a green ham like Mr Bailey's. The Marsh York ham first became popular at the end of the last century when Mr Alfred Marsh started to produce them from a factory in Brierley in Staffordshire. They are now made, following exactly the same traditional method, by Harris–Leeming Bar. The only slight difference being that they have found they are able to slightly reduce the amount of salt used.

I was lucky enough to see round the 'factory'. While modern and up to date, it is certainly not a manufacturing-type factory and the sight of literally thousands of hams hanging up to mature in their calico bags is one that I shall never forget. The hams are placed on raised wooden pallets and rubbed with a mixture of salt, saltpetre and sal prunella. They are then rubbed and turned daily for four weeks. Two or three times during the process, all the salt is washed off and a fresh salt mixture is added. Following curing, the hams are hung in a room with a slightly raised temperature until no liquid drips out. They are then put into calico bags and left to mature for approximately four months. Each ham will take a slightly different amount of time and so they are regularly inspected.

When I was talking to Mr Bailey of Scott's, he told me that his busiest times of the year were Christmas, as one would expect, and the week of the Ebor Race Meeting in York in August. This was not, as I imagined, because they were being bought up by caterers or people giving house parties. It is the gypsies, who hold a fair for

the week and buy almost as many as they can lay their hands on. In their spotless modern caravans there is only one thing they lack and that is a decent-sized refrigerator, so a ham which does not require refrigeration is ideal. They also like them as large and as fat as possible.

I have not yet had the opportunity of trying Cumberland hams which are produced at Waberthwaite by the Woodall family. They have been curing hams since 1828 and it is now run by Bar Woodall who is the seventh generation. Every report I have ever heard of them has been really excellent and I have spoken to Mrs Woodall as they have a large mail order business. They produce several varieties of ham, and one of their most popular, especially with many of the local restaurants, is an air-dried Parma type, which they have introduced comparatively recently.

There are more specialist pork butchers in the north of England than anywhere else in the British Isles. Darlington alone has eight and did have even more. It is interesting that so many of them have German names, such as Zissler, Weegnam and Funk. Apparently, one of the countless European wars caused a number of Germans to flee to England as refugees. Many of them settled in North Yorkshire where they continued with the only trade they knew, namely pork butchery. They must have had to adapt many of their recipes to conform with northern tastes, but the Germans are the greatest sausage makers in the world and this tradition has carried on through to the present generation. If you walk into one of these shops, it does not strike you that the food is at all Germanic, but it is surely no coincidence that they are amongst some of the finest pork butchers in England.

However, they are far from being the only good pork butchers. Other excellent shops I visited included Yorkshire's Oldest Pork Shop in Bradford and Buckle's in Roberttown, West Yorkshire. Ray Buckle was until recently President of the Meat and Livestock Commission and is renowned for his pork pies and roasted pig cheek. Scott's in York, in addition to selling their own and Marsh York hams, also make very good faggots, haslet and sausages. Their poloney, not usually one of my favourite pork products, was the best I have tasted anywhere.

Buckle's (above) 116 Roberttown Lane, Roberttown, West Yorkshire WF15 7LT Tel: (0924) 402594 Open 8–6 Monday to Friday, 8–1 on Saturday.

Mary's 5–6 Trinity Church Square, Richmond,
North Yorkshire DL10 HBY Tel: (0748) 4052
Open 8–6 Monday to Friday, 7–6 Saturday, 9–6 Sunday.

Weegman's (opposite) 6 Market Place,
Otley LS21 3AQ Tel: (0943) 462327
Open 8–5 Monday to Saturday.

Yorkshire's Oldest Pork Shop (opposite) 21 Ivegate,
Bradford BD1 1FQ Tel: (0274) 727987
Open 6.30–5.30 Monday to Saturday but closed Wednesday.

Zissler & Sons (opposite) 104 Bondgate, Darlington DL3 7LB
Tel: (0325) 462590
Open 8–5.30 Monday, Tuesday, Thursday, Friday, 8–4 Wedneday,
8.30–5 Saturday.

G Scott (page 96) 81 Low Petergate, York YO1 2HY
Tel: (0904) 22972 Open 6.30–5.30 Monday to Friday,
except Wednesday 6.30–2. Also mail order.

Harris–Leeming Bar (page 56) Leeming Bar, Northallerton,
Yorkshire DL7 9AW Tel (0677) 22661.
Telephone orders and mail order.

Richard Woodall (opposite) Lane End, Waberthwaite
LA19 5YJ Tel: (06577) 237 Open 8.30–5.30 Monday to
Friday, Closes 12.15–1.15. Saturday 8.30–12.
Personal shoppers and mail order.

PICKLED PORK WITH PEASE PUDDING

Pease Pudding hot
Pease Pudding cold
Pease Pudding in the pot
Nine days old

The old children's rhyme makes one realize that this was the staple diet of the poor, served up in barely differing guises day after day. Only one stage removed from the early medieval pottage or oatmeal gruel, flavoured with any vegetables and herbs that were to hand, with the occasional piece of bacon added to it, pease pudding certainly dates from the Middle Ages. It was also one of the classic dishes of the early street vendors and in the chop houses. It was a favourite dish of Queen Elizabeth I, as on her release from the Tower of London in 1558 she went straight to the London Tavern and consumed a large plate of Pork and Pease Pudding. To commemorate this event, for centuries afterwards the tavern always puts it on the menu on the anniversary of her Coronation.

Because of its connotations with poverty, pease pudding is now frequently looked upon with slight disdain, but it is good, wholesome fare and the delight of any nutritionist, being full of fibre. It is still a popular dish in the north of England and many butchers, such as Zisslers of Darlington, sell tubs of it for customers to take home and reheat.

In some parts of Northumberland pease pudding is served with roast pork, while in other areas of the country with boiled bacon, which you can use if you prefer, or may find easier to obtain. In Yorkshire it is traditional to serve pease pudding with pickled pork.

◆

1.4-kg/3-lb piece of pickled pork belly or a pickled hand of pork
weighing approximately 2.2kg/5 lb
2 onions, peeled and chopped
2 carrots, peeled and chopped
2 small turnips, peeled and chopped
About 6 peppercorns

For the pease pudding:
450g/1 lb yellow split peas, soaked overnight
1 sprig mint
50g/2 oz butter
1 egg yolk
Salt and freshly-milled black pepper

◆

Soak the pork in cold water for about 4 hours. Put into a large pan, cover with cold water and bring to the boil. Remove any scum. Add the onions, carrots and turnips and simmer gently, allowing 25 minutes to the 1 lb and 25 minutes over.

Put the peas into a muslin bag with the mint. Tie loosely with a piece of string so that there is room for the peas to expand, and add to the pan. Cook for 1½ hours. Remove from the pan. Stand in a colander and allow to drain, then empty the contents of the muslin bag and sieve into a clean pan.

Add the butter, egg yolk and seasoning and heat gently. Remove the pork from the pan and serve the pease pudding separately with the pork. It is traditional to also serve boiled cabbage and parsnips, but other vegetables complement this delicious dish very well.

Serves 6–8

PAN HAGGERTY

A Northumbrian dish, generally served for high tea. Originally one word, *Panhaggerty*, in the local dialect it means onions and potatoes, which are its main constituent. It is, however, totally impossible to make good Pan Haggerty without well-flavoured bacon fat.

◆

50g/2 oz bacon fat
900g/2 lb potatoes, peeled and very thinly sliced
2 onions, peeled and finely chopped
100g/4 oz Wensleydale cheese, grated
Salt and freshly-milled black pepper

◆

Heat the bacon fat in a large, heavy-based frying pan. Add half the potatoes, the onion and cheese, then the remaining potatoes. Season each layer well and cook over a very gentle heat for 30 minutes.

Loosen the potatoes underneath with a palette knife. Place a large plate over the frying pan, invert the potato cake on to it then slide it back into the pan. Increase the heat slightly and cook for a further 10 minutes or until browned on the underneath. Slide out of the pan on to a serving plate and serve piping hot.

Serves 4

MITTOON OF PORK

It is only in the north of England that the word mittoon has survived, but mittoons and puptons, both of which closely resembled modern terrines, were regularly served at the court of Charles II. In many of the recipes, a bread-based forcemeat is packed between layers of meat. This is rather heavy so I think this version is preferable.

◆

8 rashers streaky bacon, de-rinded
450g/1 lb pork fillet
25g/1 oz butter
1 small onion, finely chopped
100g/4 oz mushrooms, finely chopped
100g/4 oz pig's liver
100g/4 oz fat pork belly
50g/2 oz fresh white breadcrumbs
1 tablespoon brandy
1 teaspoon finely-chopped fresh thyme or ¼ teaspoon dried thyme
1 tablespoon chopped parsley
Salt and freshly-milled black pepper

◆

Place the rashers of bacon on a board and stretch them with the back of a knife. Use six of them to line the base and sides of a terrine or loaf tin.

Slit the pork fillets, place them between two sheets of damp greaseproof paper and beat with a mallet or rolling pin to flatten.

Melt the butter in a saucepan and gently fry the onion for 5 minutes. Add the mushrooms and cook for a further 4 minutes. Mince the liver and fat pork belly or process in a blender or food processor. Add to the onion and mushrooms with the remaining ingredients. Mix well.

Put a third of the minced mixture in the prepared terrine or tin and cover with half the pork fillet, then a layer of minced mixture, the remaining pork fillet and finally the last of the minced mixture. Lay the remaining bacon rashers on top.

Cover tightly with foil and a lid if available. Stand the terrine or tin in a roasting tin containing 2.5cm/1in of hot water and bake in a very moderate oven, 160°C/325°F/Gas Mark 3 for 2½ hours. Remove from the oven and stand a weight on top of the foil to press down the mittoon while it is cooling.

Serves 8–12

COLLIER'S FOOT

'She's left his foots in t'oven and they're burnt to cinders.'

Our Florrie

Also known as Lancashire Foot, this is a pasty which the miners would take with them to eat in the short 'snap' or break they were allowed while down the pit. Foot-shaped, before filling and folding, they comfortably fitted into the small oval tins they slipped into their inside pockets for their provisions.

The pastry for an authentic 'foot' was always made with bacon fat, which gave it plenty of flavour even if the filling was sometimes meagre. In these days of lean pigs it is doubtful that many people will have sufficient bacon fat for pastry-making, but lard, butter or a mixture of both can be used. The filling would vary according to what was available, but if meat was included it was bacon more often than not.

◆

175g/6 oz short crust pastry (see above and page 140)
1 tablespoon bacon fat
50g/2 oz wafer thin slices of cheese
Freshly-milled black pepper
2 large rashers collar bacon

½ teaspoon made English mustard
1 medium-sized onion, very thinly sliced
Salt
2 tablespoons beer (optional)
Beaten egg or milk for glazing

◆

Roll out the pastry to an oval approximately 20 x 22.5cm/12 x 9 in. Cut in half lengthways then roll from one end to the centre only, to give you a 'foot' shape. Brush the thick or heel ends of the pastry with the bacon fat. Lay the slices of cheese on top, dividing them between the two pasties and leaving a 0.75-cm/¼-in edge free all the way round. Season with freshly-milled black pepper. Lay a bacon rasher on each pasty and spread with mustard, then finally scatter over the onion slices and season them lightly with salt and pepper. Pour a tablespoon of beer into each one if wished.

Brush the edges of the pastry with beaten egg or milk, bring the sole or wide end of the 'foot' over the filling. Seal the edges well and place on a greased baking sheet. Brush all over with milk or beaten egg and bake in a moderately hot oven 190°C/375°F/Gas Mark 5 for 40 minutes or until golden brown. Remove from the oven and serve warm.

Makes 2

CUMBERLAND SAUCE

For many years the old ports of Cumberland carried on a thriving trade with the West Indies. Because of this there was always a plentiful supply of rum, brown sugar, spices and citrus fruits in this little corner of England. The result is some interesting regional specialities, such as Cumberland Rum Butter, Cumberland Rum Nicky (a sweet tart made of rum and dates) and the sauce that later became the classic accompaniment for hot ham, Cumberland Sauce.

As perhaps one might expect there are a number of variations to this recipe. Some include fresh or glacé cherries, others vinegar, whilst still others only use oranges rather than a combination of oranges and lemons which I find gives a pleasant touch of tartness. Once the sauce has been cooked, it can be stored in a sealed jar for several months and can then just be reheated when required.

◆

2 oranges
1 lemon
1 teaspoon made English mustard
350g/12 oz redcurrant jelly
200ml/8 fl oz port

◆

Thinly peel the rind from the oranges and lemon, then cut into matchstick strips. Bring a small pan of water to the boil, add the strips of orange and lemon peel and blanch for 1 minute, then drain. Squeeze the juice from the fruit. Put the mustard into a saucepan and gradually blend in about 2 tablespoons of the fruit juice, then add the remainder together with the jelly and port.

Put over a moderate heat until the jelly has melted, then increase the heat and boil rapidly until the mixture has reduced by a quarter. Add the orange and lemon peel and cook for a further 2 minutes.

Generally, Cumberland sauce is served hot with hot ham but it can just as well be served cold with cold ham.

Serves 10–12

CHAPTER NINE
SCOTLAND

◆

The Scots are not renowned for their pork dishes and this is largely due to their climate and terrain. Pigs do not like the cold. Even in the south of England, where it is several degrees warmer, if kept outside they need a comfortable sty for protection at night. It is possible that the original wild boars might have been able to scale heights, but even that is doubtful. One can hardly see one of today's porkers perched on the side of a precipice in the casual way that sheep seem to! Their natural habitat is lowland woodland, not the windswept highlands and so, hundreds of years ago when it all began, there would have been few pigs to domesticate.

This does not mean that no pigs at all were kept. They were generally restricted to the lowlands or border region or, when further north, to farms where they could be kept inside for six months of the year to keep them warm. The main pork and bacon producing area of Scotland is Ayrshire and from here comes the Ayrshire style of bacon. Various different kinds of cure were, and are still used. Some include the addition of beer or vinegar, but the chief difference between an Ayrshire cure and, say, a Wiltshire cure is that the rind and some of the fat is removed before curing.

Methods of butchering animals have always been different in Scotland. I used to spend about a month every summer in Fife and well remember being completely flummoxed the first time I went into a butcher's in St Andrews. Few of the cuts bore any resemblance to the familiar English ones and those that did had different names. In the south, bacon is always cut into back and streaky but in Scotland the two are kept together and form middle cut. When kept whole as a joint, it is known as Ayrshire Roll. When boiled, stuffed and then baked, it is one of the classic Scottish bacon dishes.

Vacuum-packs of Ayrshire bacon can be obtained by mail order from Highland Larder, either smoked or unsmoked, but unfortunately they do not sell joints. The Scottish tradition of smoking fish has also led to the production of some excellent smoked bacon and this can often be found in the most unlikely small grocer or butcher's shop.

The climate does not suit wheat production any better than it does pigs. Whilst some was grown, oats have always been the staple cereal, together with barley from which, of course, whisky is distilled. It is oatmeal which is the chief constituent of the Scots' white pudding which bears no relation at all either to the French *boudin blanc* or the west country's hog's pudding. In fact it contains no pork at all, which is rather confusing. White pudding consists of a mixture of oatmeal, beef suet, onions, herbs and seasonings, sometimes filled into hogs' casings.

For a country which really does not pride itself on its pork cookery and is far better known for its beef, game and fish, I was surprised to find the number of pork recipes I did.

Highland Larder (over) Room 9, Seafield House,
Seafield Road, Inverness Tel: (0463) 226410.
Mail order only.

KINGDOM OF FIFE PIE

This is a direct descendant of Shropshire Pork and Rabbit Pies, some of which used pigs' tails and/or trotters with the rabbit, others pickled pork, whilst others, as in this version, also had the addition of forcemeat balls.

Wild rabbit will give you a much stronger flavour than the domesticated variety and is preferable, but failing that, use jointed rabbit pieces which are widely available. If using a wild rabbit, the liver can be lightly fried and added to the forcemeat balls.

◆

For the filling:
1 large fresh rabbit, jointed or 650g/1½ lb rabbit joints or pieces
25g/1 oz seasoned flour
45g/1½ oz bacon fat or 25g/1 oz butter and 1 tablespoon oil
450g/1 lb shoulder pork
2 medium-sized onions, peeled and chopped
300ml/½ pt white wine
300ml/½ pt bacon, chicken or vegetable stock

2 teaspoons fresh thyme or ½ teaspoon dried thyme
Salt and freshly-milled black pepper

For the forcemeat balls:
4 rashers streaky bacon
50g/2 oz fresh white breadcrumbs
1 tablespoon chopped parsley
Grated rind ½ lemon
Salt and freshly-milled black pepper
1 egg yolk

225g/8 oz rough puff pastry (page 142)
Beaten egg for glazing

◆

Lightly toss the rabbit joints in some of the seasoned flour. Heat the bacon fat or butter and oil in a frying pan and quickly fry the joints until they are golden brown. Lift out of the pan with a fish slice and place in a 1.8-l./3-pt pie dish.

Cut the pork into 2.5-cm/1-in cubes. Toss in the seasoned flour, then add to the pan and cook until it is evenly golden. Lift out of the pan with a draining spoon and scatter over the rabbit.

Add the onion to the fat remaining in the pan and fry gently for 5 minutes. Sprinkle over the last of the flour and cook for 1 minute. Pour over the wine and the stock and bring to the boil. Stir in the thyme and seasoning then pour over the meat. Put aside.

Cut the rind off the bacon and either mince the bacon or put into a food processor. Turn into a basin and add the breadcrumbs, parsley, lemon rind and seasoning. Bind with the egg yolk. Form into walnut-sized balls and add to the pie dish. Place a pie funnel in the centre.

Roll out the pastry to an oval 2.5cm/1 in larger than the pie dish. Cut off a strip 1.25cm/½ in wide. Brush the rim of the pie dish with beaten egg and place the strip of pastry on top. Carefully lift the rolled-out pastry over the top of the pie. Seal the edges, trim, then knock up with the back of a knife and flute. Any pastry trimmings can then be rolled out and made into leaves etc., for decoration.

Brush the pie all over with beaten egg and bake in a moderately hot oven 200°C/400°F/Gas Mark 6 for 15 minutes. Lower the temperature to 180°C/350°F/Gas Mark 4 and bake for a further 1 hour. Remove from the oven and serve piping hot.

Serves 8

AYRSHIRE GALANTINE

The word 'galantine' may sound French but the dish is a British creation, referring to cold pressed meats served in their own jelly. The original galantines were always made of poultry and one thought is that the word comes from the old French *galine*, meaning chicken. By the end of the seventeenth century, a variety of meats were being used. The Victorians and Edwardians were especially fond of rather elaborate galantines in which various fowl were boned and stuffed.

This particular galantine is an extremely simple version. It can either be simply turned out of the tin and served or, if wished, it can be glazed with additional aspic jelly for a party. If you are unable to obtain any Ayrshire bacon, use a good quality unsmoked bacon instead, in which case it should first be de-rinded.

◆

550g/1¼ lb lean ground beef
225g/8 oz lean Ayrshire bacon
50g/2 oz fresh white breadcrumbs
1 tablespoon chopped parsley
1½ teaspoons chopped fresh thyme or ½ teaspoon dried thyme
Salt and freshly-milled black pepper
2 eggs, lightly beaten

◆

Tip the ground beef into a bowl. Either mince the bacon or put it into a blender or food processor. Add to the beef with all the remaining ingredients and mix well. Turn the mixture into a well-greased 650-g/1½-lb loaf tin and cover with a double layer of foil. Stand the tin in a roasting tin containing 2.5cm/1 in of hot water and bake in a very moderate oven, 160°C/325°F/Gas Mark 3 for 1½ hours. Remove the tin from the oven and place weights on top of the foil to press the galantine while it is cooling. When cold, put into the refrigerator for at least 2 hours before turning out.

To turn out, run a hot knife round the edge of the tin, then invert on to a serving dish. Serve cold with salad.

Serves 6

STUFFED AYRSHIRE ROLL

The Ayrshire roll is a great Scots speciality, consisting of a piece of middle cut bacon which contains both the back and the streaky. Ideally, of course, Ayrshire bacon should be used, but failing that, any joint of middle cut can be substituted.

◆

1.8kg/4 lb Ayrshire roll or piece of middle cut bacon
1 bay leaf
1 onion, peeled and quartered
300ml/½ pt light ale
25g/1 oz butter
100g/4 oz mushrooms, finely chopped
75g/3 oz fresh white breadcrumbs
2 tablespoons chopped parsley
1 teaspoon chopped fresh thyme or ¼ teaspoon dried thyme
Salt and freshly-milled black pepper

◆

Put the bacon to soak for 4 hours in cold water then drain. Wrap the bacon round a jam jar and tie firmly with string. Place in a large saucepan with the bay leaf, onion and ale. Cover with cold water, bring to the boil and simmer gently for 1 hour.

Remove from the pan and allow to cool for 30 minutes. Peel off any skin. While the bacon is cooling, melt the butter in a pan and fry the mushrooms gently for 5 minutes. Remove from the heat and stir in the breadcrumbs, parsley, thyme and seasoning. Mix well. Remove the jam jar and fill the cavity with the stuffing. Secure with fresh string if necessary. Make cuts about 0.75cm/¼ in apart over the fat for decoration.

Place in a roasting tin and roast in a moderately hot oven, 190°C/375°F/Gas Mark 5 for a further 1 hour. Serve hot.

Serves 8

COLLOPS

Collop comes from the French *escalope* and was a term used at one time throughout the British Isles meaning a slice of meat, bacon in particular. The Monday before Shrove Tuesday used to be known as Collop Monday, when the remains of the bacon were fried up, often accompanied by any eggs that would not be required for pancakes the following day.

In Scotland, however, the dish has always kept closer to its French origins and generally consists of slices of meat or thin minced meat patties, fried and served with a gravy.

◆

4 thin slices of pork, cut from the leg, weighing about 100g/4 oz each (in some supermarkets these may actually be called escalopes of pork)
2 tablespoons seasoned flour
25g/1 oz butter
1 tablespoon oil
1 medium-sized onion, peeled and thinly sliced
225g/8 oz button mushrooms, sliced
salt and freshly-milled black pepper
3 tablespoons Scotch whisky
6 tablespoons stock

◆

Cut the pieces of pork in half and flatten them with a meat mallet between two pieces of damp greaseproof paper. If buying escalopes, this will already have been done. Lightly coat the slices in seasoned flour. Melt the butter and oil in a large frying pan and quickly fry the meat on both sides for about 5 minutes or until golden brown. If you do not have a large enough pan, you may have to do this in two batches. Remove from the pan, put on one side and keep warm. Add the onion to the juices remaining in the pan and cook gently for about 8 minutes or until soft. Add the mushrooms and cook for a further 3 minutes. Season with salt and pepper. Replace the pork slices in the pan, pour over the whisky and stock and cook gently together for a further 5 minutes. Taste and adjust the seasoning of the sauce before serving.

Serves 4

BACON STOVIES

The word stovie is said to derive either from the French *étouffer* meaning to cook in an enclosed pot, or *éstuvier* to shut up. Either way, this method of cooking slices of potato in a covered earthenware crock has always been, and still remains, one of the most popular methods of cooking the vegetable in Scotland. Frequently they are just cooked on their own with or without an onion, but small quantities of meat and fish are sometimes added to make almost a complete meal in a pot.

◆

900g/2 lb potatoes, peeled and cut into 0.75-cm/¼-in slices
1 large onion, peeled and thinly sliced into rings
225g/8 oz streaky bacon, de-rinded and chopped
Salt and freshly-milled black pepper
Freshly-grated nutmeg
200ml/8 fl oz milk
25g/1 oz butter

◆

Well-butter a large ovenproof dish. Put a layer of potato in the bottom of the dish, cover with a few onion rings and scatter over some of the bacon. Season with a little salt (depending on how salty the bacon is), freshly-milled black pepper and nutmeg. Continue these layers, finishing with a layer of potato on the top. Pour over the milk, cover with foil and a lid and bake in a moderate oven, 180°C/350°F/Gas Mark 4 for 1½ hours. Then remove the lid, dot with the butter and bake for a further 15 minutes to brown the top.

Serves 4

CHAPTER TEN
WALES
◆

The northern part of Wales, for much the same reasons as Scotland, is not a great pork-eating part of the British Isles. However, the southern part of the Principality and the counties bordering England are. Always known as 'the little England beyond Wales', Pembrokeshire, now Dyfed, is also a good area for pigs, despite the abundance of Welsh lamb from the Prescelli hills.

Not needing access to pasture, and with a pig's ability to fatten on household scraps and other waste, meant that families in small mining communities were able to keep the animal in a stone sty or *twlc* at the bottom of the garden. According to Dorothy Hartley, the original Welsh pig was small, like other animals of Wales, and the 'cottagers' pig' to perfection. Since then he must have gone through a slight metamorphosis as the Welsh pig is now quite large and is frequently used for crossing with Large Whites and Landraces for intensive breeding and farming.

Faggots (page 44), popular throughout the British Isles, are very highly thought of in Wales, with many small butchers having their own recipes. Few of the classic Welsh recipes which use pork, other than the Welsh ciste, use it fresh. By far the majority of them use it in the form of bacon and ham, exemplifying the need to preserve as much food as possible in country areas.

The Cenarth Smokery in Dyfed is better known for its smoked fish and mutton hams than for its pork, but they also smoke bacon, ham and pork fillets. The hams and bacon are all dry-salted. They either cure these themselves or buy them in prepared and unsmoked.

Cenarth Smokery, Ffynnonddewi, Cenarth, Newcastle Emlyn, Dyfed Tel: (023987) 579.

SWP CIG MOCH

(Bacon Soup)

A good old-fashioned bacon and vegetable broth which will make a complete meal when served with crusty wholemeal bread.

◆

25g/1 oz butter or bacon fat
100g/4 oz bacon rashers, de-rinded and finely chopped
1 medium-sized potato, peeled and finely chopped
2 leeks, cleaned and finely chopped
2 sticks celery, finely chopped
900ml/1½ pt bacon, ham or vegetable stock
Salt and freshly-milled black pepper

◆

Melt the butter or bacon fat in a pan, add the bacon and cook for about 5 minutes. Then add the vegetables and toss together for 5 minutes. Pour over the stock, cover, bring to the boil and simmer gently for 30 minutes. Taste and adjust the seasoning.

Serves 4–6

POTTED HAM

Potted meats were considered to be an almost essential part of a Victorian breakfast, together with sausages, bacon and eggs, cold ham and, of course, a slice or two of cold game. In his travelogue *Wild Wales*, published in 1862, George Borrow described a breakfast he had enjoyed at an inn as follows: 'What a breakfast! Pot of hare; ditto of trout; pot of prepared shrimps; tin of sardines; beautiful beefsteak; eggs, mutton, large loaf and butter, not forgetting capital tea. There's a breakfast for you!'

This potted ham makes very clever use of the ham fat, which is often discarded as being useless. Many potted meats combine the ham with butter but the ham fat, when finely minced, gives added flavour as well as the necessary moisture to the finished dish. While the best potted ham will be achieved by using the best quality hams, this is also a good way of using up a piece of cooked bacon forehock or shoulder.

450g/1 lb cooked ham
175g/6 oz ham fat
1 small onion, finely grated
½ teaspoon ground mace
3 tablespoons brandy
Freshly-milled black pepper
Salt, if necessary
100g/4 oz clarified butter (see below)

Either very finely mince the ham and ham fat or put into a blender or food processor and process until quite smooth. Beat the onion into the mixture with the mace, brandy and pepper. Taste and season with a little salt if necessary. Pack into a pot and cover with clarified butter if wishing to store. Otherwise, cover with clingfilm and keep in the refrigerator for 3–4 days. Serve as a starter with hot toast.

Serves 8

BRITHYLL A CIG MOCH

No chapter or book on Welsh cooking would be complete without this classic Welsh recipe for trout and bacon. Some recipes suggest lining the dish with bacon, placing the trout on top and then covering with more bacon. I think perhaps it is easier to simply wrap the bacon round the trout, then you do not have to worry so much about quantities.

For each trout weighing about 275g/10 oz you will need:
Salt and freshly-milled black pepper
A squeeze of lemon
About 2 teaspoons chopped parsley
2 large rashers smoked streaky bacon

Clean the fish if this has not already been done. Season each one inside and out with salt and freshly-milled black pepper. Squeeze over some lemon juice and sprinkle with parsley. De-rind the bacon and wrap two rashers round each trout, starting from just below the head.

Put into a buttered ovenproof dish and bake in a moderately hot oven, 200°C/400°F/Gas Mark 6 for about 20 minutes. The bacon should be nicely crisp and the fish just cooked through. Do not overcook it or the fish can become dry.

BACON WITH LAVERBREAD

My children have never forgotten the one and only time when, several years ago, I tried this combination – the most celebrated Welsh breakfast dish. Having heard people talk about laverbread (which, for the uninitiated, is minced, boiled seaweed) with enthusiasm, and regularly witnessed people collecting it on the Pembrokeshire beaches we frequented, I felt the time had come to try this delicacy. I found some without difficulty in Haverfordwest market and dutifully wrote down exactly how it had to be cooked.

The children rejected my offer to share this treat and opted for cornflakes but I duly set about making my own fare. I fried the bacon in the pan until it was crisp, removed it from the pan, added the laverbread to the fat remaining, fried it and then added it to the bacon on the plate. By this stage, my enthusiasm was starting to diminish. The almost black mass next to the bacon did not look very appetizing. I dug my fork into it and lifted it to my mouth. Apparently the look on my face was a picture. I have never tasted anything I disliked so intensely. It was like pure iodine!

Needless to say, I then procceeded to eat all the bacon to take the taste away and discarded the rest of the laverbread in the bin. Clearly, it is an acquired taste which I am never going to acquire!

It is with difficulty, therefore, that I recommend this delicacy. However, if you have never tried it, you may wish to be brave and experiment. As it is not expensive, if you do not like it, vast sums have not been squandered. Fresh laverbread is obtainable in Haverfordwest market held on Fridays, Carmarthen market on Wednesdays and Saturdays and every day in Swansea market. It is also available both fresh and canned from some health food stores both in Wales and other parts of the British Isles. Sometimes it also has the addition of a little fine oatmeal and many people find this holds its shape better and is easier to fry.

WELSH CISTE

Ciste is Welsh for coffin, the original name for any pie. At one time, with the limited cooking equipment available, all the pies made were raised pies. One can only presume that they were frequently raised round a rectangular block, hence the name.

Lack of equipment, and in particular an oven, would also explain the origins of this dish. It is effectively a pie cooked in a saucepan and in itself forms a complete meal. Its practicality has made it popular not only in Wales but throughout the north of England, as well as across the water to their Celtic neighbours, the Irish, where it is almost a national dish.

◆

6 lean pork chops
3 pigs' kidneys
2 leeks, sliced
4 carrots, peeled and sliced
1 tablespoon chopped parsley
1 teaspoon dried thyme
50g/2 oz sultanas
Salt and freshly-milled black pepper
600ml/1 pt stock
225g/8 oz suet pastry (page 141)

◆

Put the pork chops round the edge of a saucepan. Slice the kidneys, discarding the cores, and put into the centre of the pan together with the leeks, carrots, parsley, thyme and sultanas. Season with salt and pepper. Pour over the stock, cover the pan and simmer gently for 30 minutes. Taste and adjust the seasoning of the stock. Roll out the pastry to a circle large enough to fit the saucepan and place on top of the meat and stock, but allow the top of the chops to poke through. Cover with a tightly-fitting lid allowing the pastry to expand and cook for a further 1½ hours.

Remove from the heat and cut into six wedges so that everyone has a chop together with the kidney and vegetables.

Serves 6

FEEST Y CYBDD

(The Miser's Feast)

This is an old dish from Carmarthen, so called because it was said that the miser would eat the bacon-flavoured potatoes and onions for one meal and reserve the actual bacon to serve with plain boiled potatoes the following day.

◆

650g/1½ lb potatoes, peeled and thinly sliced
2 large onions, peeled and thinly sliced
600ml/1 pt stock or water
225–350g/8–12 oz sliced bacon rashers (collar is ideal for this)
2 tablespoons chopped parsley

◆

Layer the potatoes and onions in a saucepan. Pour over the stock or water and bring to the boil. If using water, it may be necessary to add some salt. However, with stock this may not be necessary and should be used with caution so the end dish is not too salty.

Place the bacon rashers on the top, cover and simmer very gently for about 1 hour. By this time the potatoes should be cooked through and most of the liquid absorbed. Sprinkle with parsley before serving.

Serves 4

CAWL

The national dish of Wales, Cawl varies considerably not only from family to family but according to the time of year and what is available. The garnish of finely-shredded raw leek, however, remains fairly constant as does the practice of accompanying it with wholemeal bread and some cheese.

There are two ways of serving it. It can be carried to the table in a large bowl and everybody is then served with a portion of the meat and vegetables together with the broth in large soup bowls. Alternatively, it can be eaten like the French *pot-au-feu*, with the broth being eaten first like soup, followed by the meat and vegetables.

Cawl is frequently reheated the following day, with a few extra fresh vegetables, such as shredded cabbage, being added. It then becomes known as Cawl Aildwyn or Twice-Heated Broth.

◆

1 tablespoon lard, beef dripping or bacon fat
900-g/2-lb piece of brisket of beef
2 large onions, peeled and chopped
2 parsnips, peeled and chopped
2 carrots, peeled and chopped
1 medium-sized swede, peeled and coarsely chopped
675-g/1½-lb piece of bacon collar
1 bouquet garni
2 sprigs thyme
1.2 l./2 pt water, meat or vegetable stock
450g/1 lb potatoes
Salt and freshly-milled black pepper
3 leeks, preferably young thin ones, very finely chopped to garnish

◆

Heat the fat in a pan, add the brisket and brown quickly. Remove from the pan and put on one side. Add the onion, parsnips, carrots and swede to the pan and cook gently for about 5 minutes. Replace the beef together with the bacon, bouquet garni and thyme. Add the water or stock. Cover and bring to the boil. Reduce the heat and simmer gently for 2½ hours.

Peel the potatoes and cut into 1.25-cm/½-in pieces. Add to the pan and simmer gently for a further 30 minutes. Taste and adjust the seasoning. Turn into a large serving dish or individual bowls and scatter over the finely-chopped leeks just before serving.

Serves 6–8

CHAPTER ELEVEN
BRITISH HERITAGE

◆

In a book such as this it was inevitable that there would be some recipes which were commonly made throughout the British Isles but did not have any regional bias. Without recipes for such dishes as Roast Suckling Pig, Pork 'n' Beans, Devilled Kidneys and Pork Galantine, this book would have been incomplete. Equally there were others which not only taste good but have such a fascinating story behind them that I wanted to include them.

ROAST SUCKLING PIG

Unquestionably, this is pork at its very best and it is unfortunate that it is so rarely served in Britain these days. The meat is sweet, succulent, beautifully tender and there is virtually no fat on it at all. True, it is quite expensive, but not in comparison with other speciality meats such as goose, wild duck or even fillet steak and, other than the bones, there is no waste. There is also the added advantage that it will feed about twenty-five people very comfortably.

I think there are probably two reasons for its lack of popularity. Firstly, there is the problem of finding an oven big enough to cook it in and secondly, the sight of a life-like, though dead, piglet can be very off-putting. I managed to solve these two problems simultaneously when I cooked one for a Christmas party. The one my butcher obtained for me weighed about 11kg/25 lb, and it was fairly obvious that it was not going to fit into my normal domestic oven without cutting it in two. This is a common practice in parts of Europe where it is eaten regularly, but you then do not have a spare shelf for roasting the potatoes and also there is a slight danger of it becoming dry.

Consequently, I cut off the head, tail and trotters and when this was done, by curling it round to the shape of the roasting tin, it just fitted. Doing this immediately made it look much like any other joint of meat, which relieved me. I am not squeamish but, being rather sentimental about pigs, I felt guilty when it was whole and a great deal better once it had been dismembered.

One of the great delights of suckling pig is the crackling. There is plenty of it and, because the skin is thinner than in an older pig, when it is crisp it is not nearly as difficult to eat. There is one disadvantage to my method of roasting which had the pig lying on its side. That is, even though I first made it crisp and then turned it over to crisp the other side, it still became slightly soft. To obtain the maximum amount of crisp crackling, you really do need to cook it on its belly but this requires a larger oven. Even better, spit roast it, but this is a rarely feasible or practical idea. Should you find that the crackling has become a little soft, you can always strip it off in one piece and put it under a moderate grill where it will successfully re-crisp.

In order to obtain crisp crackling, it is important to score the skin properly. Either use a really good sharp knife or, better still, if you can get hold of one, use a scalpel. As evenly as you can, score the skin into strips about 0.75cm/¼ in wide all over, including between the legs and right down to the belly cavity. The pig is then ready for stuffing.

The most usual stuffing is sage and onion. These quantities will provide plenty of stuffing for twenty-five people, although it will not completely fill the body cavity.

---◆---

Sage and Onion Stuffing
1.2kg/3 lb onions
450g/1 lb fresh white breadcrumbs
4 tablespoons chopped fresh sage or 1 tablespoon dried sage
100g/4 oz butter, melted
Salt and freshly-milled black pepper

---◆---

Peel the onions, put into a pan of boiling salted water and cook for 30 minutes. Drain, and when cool enough to handle, either chop finely by hand or put into a blender or food processor. Combine with the breadcrumbs and sage and mix lightly. Stir in the butter, then season to taste with salt and pepper.

Pack the stuffing into the belly cavity of the pig. If you are going to spit roast it, you will then need to sew together the two flaps of the belly to secure the stuffing, but otherwise this is not necessary. Lay the pig on a rack in a roasting tin, brush all over with a little oil and sprinkle with salt. Roast in a moderately hot oven, 190°C/375°F/Gas Mark 5 for 4 hours. Halfway through cooking, using a clean pair of thick oven gloves, carefully lift the pig on to a working surface. Pour off all the fat and juices which have collected in the pan, then turn the pig over and replace in the oven.

Owing to the size of the pig, it generates quite a large amount of steam and, depending on the type of oven, this can prevent the crackling from crisping. If this happens, simply increase the oven temperature to 220°C/425°F/Gas Mark 7 for the last 30 minutes.

Remove from the oven and leave covered with a clean tea towel for 5 minutes before carving.

Gravy

Once the fat and juices have been taken from the pan halfway through cooking, the gravy can be started. As the meat juices which form are extremely rich, they need to be used with a little caution. About six tablespoons will be plenty to give a really meaty gravy. Any more will make it just too rich and for this reason it is suggested to use water from cooking the vegetables, rather than meat stock.

◆

4 tablespoons dripping from cooking the pork
4 tablespoons flour
6 tablespoons meat juices from the pork
6 tablespoons sweet sherry
900ml/1½ pt liquor from cooking vegetables
Salt and freshly-milled black pepper

◆

Heat the dripping in a pan, then stir in the flour. Cook over a very low heat for about 10 minutes or until the flour is a good golden brown. Remove from the heat and gradually stir in the meat juices and sherry. Just before serving, when the vegetables are cooked, stir in the vegetable liquor. Heat gently and season to taste. Serve with the pork.

Baked Apples with Apricot

These make a really good accompaniment to roast suckling pig. If you have access to another oven, the potatoes can be cooked in that. The baked apples can then be put under the pig for the last 45 minutes cooking.

◆

2 x 350-g/12-oz jars apricot preserve
Juice of 2 lemons
12–13 medium-sized cooking apples

◆

Tip the apricot preserve into a basin and stir in the lemon juice. Core the apples, place in a roasting tin and divide the apricot preserve between them, spooning it down into the cavity where the core was removed. Pour a little water into the roasting tin so that it comes about 1.25cm/½ inch up the apples. Place in a moderately hot oven, 190°C/375°F/Gas Mark 5 for 45 minutes. Remove from the oven and lift out of the pan. Place on a large serving platter, then cut each one in half. Serve half an apple with each portion of suckling pig.

Serves 24–26

CROWN ROAST OF PORK

Whilst a crown of lamb may be better known, a crown roast of pork is even more spectacular. It will serve twelve to fourteen people, which makes it an excellent dish for a large dinner party. Make sure your butcher gives you the rind so that you have crackling to serve with the meat. Either ask him to score it or do this yourself. He should also give you the bones which can be boiled up to make stock for gravy.

◆

Crown of pork made with 12–14 loin chops

For the stuffing
25g/1 oz butter
100g/4 oz bacon, de-rinded and finely chopped
2 sticks celery, finely chopped
1 cooking apple, peeled, cored and finely chopped
1 large onion, peeled and finely chopped
175g/6 oz fresh wholemeal breadcrumbs
2 teaspoons chopped fresh sage or ½ teaspoon dried sage
2 tablespoons chopped parsley
4 tablespoons dry cider
Salt and freshly-milled black pepper

◆

Melt the butter in a pan, add the bacon, celery, apple and onion and cook gently for 10 minutes. Remove from the heat, stir in the breadcrumbs, sage, parsley, cider and seasoning.

Place the crown in a roasting tin and cover the ends of the bones with foil. Fill the crown with the stuffing and cover this with foil. Place the scored rind in the roasting tin. Roast in a moderately hot oven, 190°C/375°F/Gas Mark 5 for 2½ hours. Remove the foil from the stuffing for the last 30 minutes.

Serves 12–14

DEVILLED KIDNEYS

The art of devilling food, or giving dishes a hot, sharp flavour, was started by the Georgians, though possibly perfected by the Victorians. Their popularity as a breakfast dish is doubtless explained by the fact that they were thought to be a hangover cure. In his *Cook's Oracle* published in 1817, Dr Kitchiner wrote, 'Every man must have experienced that when he has got deep into his third bottle. . . his stomach is seized with a certain craving which seems to demand a stimulant. The provocatives used on such an occasion an ungrateful world has combined to term devils.'

◆

450g/1 lb pigs' kidneys
45g/1½ oz flour
50g/2 oz butter
1 large onion, peeled and chopped
150ml/¼ pt beef stock
2 teaspoons made English mustard
1 tablespoon Worcestershire sauce
3 anchovy fillets, finely chopped
Freshly-milled black pepper and salt, if necessary
2 tablespoons chopped parsley to garnish

◆

Cut the kidneys into 1.25-cm/½-in pieces, discarding the core. Toss in the flour. Melt the butter in a pan, add the onion and fry gently for 5 minutes. Increase the heat slightly, add the kidneys and cook for a further 5 minutes, stirring frequently. Pour in the beef stock blended with the mustard and Worcestershire sauce and bring to the boil, stirring all the time. Reduce the heat, stir in the anchovies and simmer gently for a further 10 minutes, stirring from time to time. Taste and adjust the seasoning, adding salt if necessary.

Turn into a serving dish and sprinkle with the chopped parsley. If serving for breakfast, it is traditional to accompany with hot toast or croûtons of fried bread or serve with potatoes and vegetables.

Serves 4

ANGELS ON HORSEBACK

This classic Victorian savoury was traditionally served at the end of a meal. When encountered these days, it is more likely to be as a cocktail canapé. Other variations include small queen scallops and mussels which can be equally as good and are considerably less strain on the wallet!

◆

12 oysters
Lemon juice
Cayenne pepper
12 rashers streaky bacon, de-rinded
Buttered toast (see method)

◆

Thoroughly clean the oysters, squeeze a little lemon juice over them and season with cayenne pepper. Wrap a rasher of bacon round each oyster and secure with a cocktail stick. Grill for about 5 minutes under a hot grill, turning once until the bacon is just cooked through. Do not overcook or the oysters will spoil. Serve hot, either as a cocktail snack or place three angels on a piece of buttered toast and serve at once.

Serves 4 as a savoury or makes 12 cocktail snacks

DEVILS ON HORSEBACK

As one might expect, in contrast to the white of the oysters, the devils are always black! They are either in the form of a prune stuffed with a blanched almond or chutney, or a piece of chicken or turkey liver with the bacon wrapped round and grilled.

POTTED PORK

There are two ways in which meat can be potted. Either cooked meat is ground down to a paste with butter, seasoned with herbs and spices, packed into a pot and covered with clarified butter as in the Potted Ham on page 117. Or, in recipes such as the one below which closely resembles French pâtés and terrines, the raw meat is packed tightly into a pot, covered with stock or wine and then cooked very slowly in the oven before being covered with clarified butter or lard. This was essential, as the main purpose of potting was to preserve the food. A thick covering of butter or lard poured over immediately it was cooked prevented air, and consequently bacteria, from entering.

An interesting variation of potted meat is beef cheese, which was a standard provision on board ship. Finely-chopped beef, together with bacon and plenty of beef suet, herbs and spices, was cooked in an earthenware pot or a tin lined with bacon. The fat from the suet and the bacon rose to the surface to provide an airtight seal. The entire dish was then covered with flour and water or suet huff pastry, baked in the oven and then allowed to cool overnight to provide a double protection. Once cold and set, this beef cheese could be kept on board for several months before opening.

◆

450g/1 lb fat belly pork
450g/1 lb lean pork shoulder
½ teaspoon ground mace
2 cloves garlic, crushed
6 juniper berries, crushed
3 anchovy fillets, finely chopped
Salt and freshly-milled black pepper
150ml/¼ pt dry white wine
100g/4 oz clarified butter (optional)

◆

Remove the skin and any bones from the belly pork and chop finely together with the pork shoulder. Put into a bowl, add the mace, garlic, juniper berries, anchovies and seasoning and mix well. Pack into a 1.2-l./2-pt dish and pour over the wine. Cover the dish first with a layer of foil and then a lid. Bake in a very moderate oven 150°C/300°F/Gas Mark 2 for 3 hours. Remove from the oven and stand a weight on top to press the meat while it is cooling. Once cold, the pork can be covered with clarified butter if you wish to store it. Otherwise, simply serve cold with fresh crusty bread, either as a starter or as a main course.

Serves 6–8

PORK 'N' BEANS

One of the countryman's great staples, not only in Britain but throughout Europe. One has only to think of French Cassoulet. This was also a recipe that went to America with the Pilgrim Fathers and came back to us as Boston Baked Beans! During the autumn, fresh pork might have been used, but usually it was pickled pork. Then, as winter progressed and supplies became shorter, bacon was substituted. When bacon was used, the beans were often cooked separately so that the end result was not too salty. The contrast that existed for so many centuries in the diet between rich and poor is exemplified in a story about a visit George III made during the building of Woolwich Arsenal. Whilst there, he was given a plate of pork 'n' beans from a pot kept over an open fire. So entranced was he by this staple food that he demanded that he be served it as often as possible. A command which doubtless caused much scratching of heads in the royal kitchens.

Garlic rarely features in British cookery, although it was a well known and popular flavouring in Elizabethan times. Shakespeare, after all, advised his 'most dear actors' to 'eat no onions nor garlic for we are to utter sweet breath.' Certainly, to my mind, the pungency of garlic improves this dish enormously.

◆

450g/1 lb haricot beans
900-g/2-lb piece of salt pork
2 cloves garlic, crushed
2 onions, finely chopped
1 teaspoon dried mixed herbs
1.2 l./2 pt water or stock
Salt and freshly-milled black pepper

◆

Soak the beans overnight in cold water and soak the pork for about 4 hours. Drain both. Put the beans into a fireproof casserole with the garlic, onion and herbs, pour over the stock or water and bring to the boil. Boil rapidly for 10 minutes, then remove from the heat and add the pork. Put into a low oven, 160°C/325°F/Gas Mark 3 and leave for 3 hours. Taste and adjust the seasoning before serving.

Serves 4–6

GALANTINE OF PORK

One of the great advantages of galantines (page 111) is that it is a way of making some of the cheaper cuts of meat into feasts fit for a king, as this recipe proves.

◆

For the stock
2 pigs' trotters, split
2 onions, peeled and roughly chopped
2 carrots
300ml/½ pt white wine
900ml/1½ pt water
1 bay leaf
Salt and freshly-milled black pepper

For the galantine
1 hand of pork, boned
1 cooked pig's tongue or 225g/8 oz cooked ox tongue
450g/1 lb lean pork belly
450g/1 lb veal
225g/8 oz large mushrooms
2 cloves garlic, crushed
4 tablespoons chopped parsley
¼ teaspoon grated nutmeg
¼ teaspoon ground cinnamon
Salt and freshly-milled black pepper

◆

Put all the ingredients for the stock into a pan, bring to the boil, remove any scum, then simmer gently for 1 hour.

Lay out the hand of pork on a working surface. Mince the tongue, pork belly, veal and mushrooms. Add the remaining ingredients and mix well. Spread evenly over the pork then roll up and tie with string. Tie the meat up in a piece of muslin, add to the stock, cover the pan and simmer very gently for 3 hours. Remove and allow to cool in the stock for a while. Then lift out the pork and remove the muslin and string. Place in a dish and strain over just enough of the stock to fill the dish. Press down with a plate and weights then leave overnight. Serve sliced.

Serves 10–12

CHAPTER TWELVE
LOOKING AHEAD
◆

Food and cookery does not stand still but is perpetually changing and developing. Over the past few years, a new kind of British cookery has evolved in which the very best British ingredients are used to make the most superb simple food. With the influence of the great French masters of Nouvelle Cuisine, it is a style which is quintessentially British.

The best promoters of this food are the chefs in many of our country restaurants. Some of them have very kindly contributed recipes for this chapter, for which the publishers and I are extremely grateful. They come from various areas and, wherever possible, have used produce from their own locality. These recipes are likely to become the regional dishes of the future.

Midsummer House, Midsummer Common, Cambridge CB4 1HA
Tel: (0223) 69299.

Bradfield House Restaurant, Bradfield Combust,
Bury St Edmunds, Suffolk IP30 OLR
Tel: (028 486) 301.

Kenward's Restaurant, Pipe Passage, 151a High Street,
Lewes, Sussex BN7 1XU
Tel: Lewes 472343.

White's Restaurant, 93 High Street, Cricklade, Wiltshire
Tel: (0793) 751110.

MIDSUMMER HOUSE TENDERLOIN OF PORK WITH BLUEBERRIES

Midsummer House, in the former common-keeper's cottage on Midsummer Common in Cambridge, has recently been selected as The Good Food Guide's Cambridge Newcomer of the Year. This recipe was devised by their chef, Jackie Rae.

◆

2 pork tenderloins
Salt and freshly-milled black pepper
Oil or dripping
150ml/¼ pt port
150ml/¼ pt chicken stock
225g/8 oz blueberries (see note)
300ml/½ pt double cream
Sprig of parsley

◆

Trim the pork of any fat, remove the outer skin and season. Heat the oil or dripping in an ovenproof pan and lightly brown the pork. Place in a moderately hot oven, 200°C/400°F/Gas Mark 6 for approximately 10–15 minutes until just firm to the touch. The pork should be slightly pink in the centre. Keep warm.

Meanwhile, heat the pork then add the stock and a few blueberries. Reduce the liquid by two-thirds. Add the cream, bring to the boil and simmer for approximately 10 minutes. Remove the fat from the pan in which the pork was cooked, then deglaze with the sauce. Strain. Heat the remaining blueberries in a little stock syrup.

To assemble the dish, slice the tenderloin, pour the sauce on to the plates then arrange the slices of pork on the sauce. Garnish with the blueberries and a sprig of parsley.

NOTE: This dish is equally as good with fresh brambles.

Serves 4

BRADFIELD HOUSE PORK FILLETS WITH PRUNES AND CHICKEN LIVERS

Mrs Victoria Stephenson is a wonderful cook who owns and runs Bradfield House Restaurant near Bury St Edmunds with her husband Michael. They grow many of their own vegetables and have a prolific herb garden with many of the old English herbs such as lovage and sorrel. The Sunday lunch I had there a couple of years ago was superb. Not only was the food magnificent but the atmosphere was wonderfully relaxed. You can even sit down in the bar or drawing room with your coffee after lunch and devour the Sunday papers!

◆

2 pork fillets
225g/8 oz chicken livers
A little butter
6 prunes, soaked and stoned
About 100g/4 oz breadcrumbs
1 egg
About 5 finely-chopped basil leaves
6 rashers sweetcure bacon
Marsala and crème fraiche (see below)

◆

Cut the pork fillets down the middle and flatten. Stiffen the chicken livers in a little butter. Chop the livers and prunes and combine with the breadcrumbs, egg and basil. Stuff the pork fillets. Flatten out the bacon with a broad knife and wrap around the pork fillets. Secure with a bit of string. Roast in a hot oven, 200°C/400°F/Gas Mark 6 for about 45 minutes. When cooked, deglaze the pan juices with Marsala and crème fraiche. Cut the fillets at a slant. Put the sauce on warm plates and place the pork on top. Serve with watercress and new potatoes. Victoria Stephenson likes to serve salad with this dish as it cuts the richness of the sauce.

Serves 4

KENWARD'S LOIN OF PORK WITH ORANGE AND GINGER

Almost all the pork that John Kenward serves at his restaurant in Lewes in Sussex comes from Elaine Liddle's farm at nearby Chelwood Gate. Her small farm is Soil Association approved and he particularly likes the pork from her Tamworth pigs.

Bone a loin of pork, remove the skin and some fat. Make a stock with trimmings, bones, etc. Cut meat into generous 'chops' about 30mm thick and marinate in cider and orange juice. All this can be done a day or two ahead and it is in fact probably better to do it this way; the marinade can improve the meat and the fat is much easier to remove from stock when it is cool.

Slice very thinly some peeled fresh ginger. About 5 slices per 'chop'. Cut each 'chop' between the fat and eye and insert a sliver of ginger. Bake in a hot oven 10–15 mins, until lean meat is firm and outer fat has browned slightly. Meanwhile put on stock to reduce, add juice of ½ orange per chop and the rest of the ginger; no other seasoning should be needed. Slice each chop into two or three and pour sauce around. Sauce should be almost syrupy; the only adjustment may be a little lemon juice depending upon the acidity of the oranges used. A few strips of orange zest make the dish look good.

WHITE'S ELIZABETHAN PORK

White's in Cricklade, Wiltshire, was awarded the title Wiltshire Restaurant of the Year by *The Good Food Guide* in 1988. Colin White says 'the restaurant prides itself on its use of the finest ingredients which, in the case of meat, especially pork, means free range. Local producers, usually smallholders, are encouraged to rear for us, the snag being that we have to take at least half the pig. This taxes our ingenuity to the full in using the forend, head, etc. Hence the menu might feature brawn (pork cheese in your neck of the woods I believe!), cassoulet, paella and this delightfully old-fashioned-tasting stew.'

1.1kg/3 lb shoulder pork cut into cubes
Olive oil for frying
2 medium-sized onions, thinly sliced
1 head celery, thinly sliced
¾ bottle red wine (a robust one is best)
1 lemon, thinly-grated zest and juice
1 orange, thinly-grated zest and juice
1 large cooking apple, peeled and sliced
100g/4 oz fresh dates, peeled, stoned and coarsely chopped
100g/4 oz raisins
100g/4 oz walnuts, broken-up lightly
1 teaspoon quatre epices (pepper, nutmeg, allspice, ginger)
1 teaspoon curry powder
Salt to taste
2 tablespoons honey
Piece of pork skin to place on top of the meat for extra succulence

Fry the pork in the olive oil to seal and brown lightly. Remove to a casserole. Fry the onion and celery until golden. Deglaze the pan with the wine. Remove to the casserole and add all the other ingredients. Place the piece of pork skin on top. Cover and simmer 1½ hours.

BASIC PASTRY RECIPES

The following are the basic pastry recipes which have been used throughout this book.

SHORT CRUST PASTRY

225g/8 oz plain flour
A good pinch salt
100g/4 oz butter or margarine, or a mixture of margarine and lard
About 2 tablespoons cold water

Sift the flour and salt into a bowl. Rub in the fat until the mixture resembles fine breadcrumbs. Using a fork, mix in the water until the dough clings together and forms a firm dough. Turn on to a lightly-floured surface and knead lightly until smooth.
Use as directed in the recipe.

NOTE: 175g/6 oz short crust pastry in a recipe refers to pastry made with 175g/6 oz flour and 75g/3 oz fat, etc.

CHEESE PASTRY

Make up the pastry as above, but add 50g/2 oz finely-grated strong Cheddar cheese to every 225g/8 oz flour after the fat has been rubbed into the flour. Mix in thoroughly, then add the water and continue as above.

SUET CRUST PASTRY

◆

225g/8 oz self-raising flour or 225g/8 oz plain flour and 2 teaspoons baking powder
½ teaspoon salt
100g/4 oz shredded beef suet
About 150ml/¼ pt cold water

◆

Sift together the flour, baking powder, if using, and salt into a bowl. Stir in the suet then, using a fork, bind with the water to form a soft dough. Turn on to a lightly-floured surface and knead lightly.
Use as directed in the recipe.

HOT WATER CRUST PASTRY

◆

350g/12 oz plain flour
1 teaspoon salt
125g/5 oz lard
150ml/¼ pt water

◆

Sift the flour and salt together into a mixing bowl. Cut the lard into about 4 pieces and put into a pan with the water. Place over a moderate heat and bring gradually to the boil. As soon as the mixture boils, pour it immediately into the centre of the flour. Beat well with a wooden spoon until the mixture clings together in a ball, leaving the sides of the basin clean. When cool enough to handle, place on a lightly-floured surface and knead lightly until smooth. Use as directed in the recipe.

QUICK ROUGH PUFF PASTRY

◆

225g/8 oz plain flour
A pinch salt
175g/6 oz butter or 75g/3 oz margarine and 75g/3 oz lard
Just under 150ml/¼ pt water

◆

Sift the flour and salt into a mixing bowl. Cut the fat up roughly, and add to the bowl. Using two round-bladed knives in a scissor action, cut the fat into pieces about 0.75-cm/¼-in square. Add the water and mix to a soft dough.

Roll out the dough to a rectangle approximately 30cm x 12.5cm/ 12 x 5 in. Bring the top third of the pastry down and the bottom third of the pastry up to make an envelope shape. Turn the pastry at a right angle and roll out again. Repeat this rolling and folding three more times. Cover and put into the refrigerator to rest for at least 30 minutes. Use as directed in the recipe.

BIBLIOGRAPHY

Acton, E., *Modern Cooking In All Its Branches: Reduced To An Easy Practice* (1845)

Ayrton, E., *English Provincial Cooking* (Mitchell Beazley, London, 1980)

Ayrton, E., *The Cookery of England* (André Deutsch, London, 1974)

Beeton, I., *Book of Household Management* (Ward Lock, London, 1861)

Boyd, L. (ed.), *British Cookery* (Croom Helm, London, 1976)

Cobbett, W., *Cottage Economy* (1821, republished 1978)

Downing, E., *Keeping Pigs* (Pelham Books, London, 1978)

Farmhouse Cookery (Reader's Digest, London, 1980)

Fitzgibbon, T., *The Food of the Western World* (Hutchinson, London, 1976)

Grigson, J., *Charcuterie and French Cookery* (Michael Joseph, London, 1967)

Grigson, J., *The Observer Guide to British Cookery* (Michael Joseph, London, 1984)

Hartley, D., *Food in England* (1954, republished Futura, London, 1985)

Hippisley Coxe, A. & A., *Antony and Araminta Hippisley-Coxe's Book of Sausages* (1978, revised Victor Gollancz, London, 1987)

Innes, J., *The Country Kitchen* (Frances Lincoln, 1979)

Lofts, N., *Domestic Life in England* (Weidenfeld & Nicolson, London, 1976)

Millon, M. & K., *The Taste of Britain* (Webb & Bower, London, 1985)

Smith, D., (ed.), *The Good Food Guide* (Consumers Association, London)

Smith, D., & Mabey, D., (ed.), *The Good Food Directory* (Consumers Association, London, 1986)

Wilson, C., *Food and Drink in Britain* (Constable, London, 1973)

Wiseman, J., *A History of the British Pig* (Duckworth, London, 1986)

INDEX

◆